THE WAITE GROUP®

P9-ELX-729

Walkthroughs

AND

Flybys CD

OVER 500
MEGABYTES
OF THE
BEST ANIMATED PRESENTATIONS

Phil Shatz

WAITE GROUP
PRESS™

Publisher • *Mitchell Waite*
Editorial Director • *Scott Calamar*
Managing Editor • *Joel Fugazzotto*
Production Director • *Julianne Ososke*
Design • *Cecile Kaufman*
Technical Coordinator • *David Middleton*
Production • *LeeAnn Nelson*
Illustration • *Pamela Drury-Wattenmaker*

© 1993 by The Waite Group®, Inc.

Published by Waite Group Press™, 200 Tamal Plaza, Corte Madera, CA 94925.

Waite Group Press™ is distributed to bookstores and book wholesalers by Publishers Group West, Box 8843, Emeryville, CA 94662, 1-800-788-3123 (in California 1-510-658-3453).

Library of Congress-in-Publication Data
Shatz, Phil
　　　Walkthroughs and flybys CD : over 500 megabytes of the best
　　animated presentations / Phil Shatz.
　　　　　　p.　　　　cm.
　　Includes bibliographical references and index.
　　　ISBN 0-18-783926-3 : $29.95
　　　1. Computer graphics.　　2. Multimedia systems.　　I. Title
　　t385.S42　1993
　　741.5"8--dc20

For Carolyn

*Her patience and love
warms my heart and comforts my soul.*

Dedication

Walkthroughs & Flybys CD is dedicated to aspiring computer artists everywhere. As Waite Group Press would like to continue to bring you the best in PC multimedia, it is our hope that this volume will generate a flood of contributions for the next book in the series. For more information read "Guidelines for Contributing Your Work," which you will find in the Credits section of the menu system.

ACKNOWLEDGMENTS

The author owes a debt of gratitude to many in the creation of this book. As you will see in the Credits section of the CD, there are over 100 people who directly contributed their work, skills, or advice to this project. Certain people, however, made such significant efforts that I am glad to have this opportunity to publicly thank them.

The early support from Bob Bennett, Simon Hodson, and Gary Yost at Autodesk were all crucial to getting this project off the ground. Special thanks go to Jason Gibbs for his valuable advice and the loan of equipment. As a beta site, contributor, and friend he really pulled out all the stops. Nick Corston was a savior for making his Philips CDD452 machine available during the final stages of mastering.

Working with Waite Group Press has been a fantastic experience. With the mountains of electronic mail, FEDEX® packages, and gold write-once CDs behind us, I want to thank the whole crew for their support and hard work. Particularly, I have to thank Mitch, because without his drive, perception, and belief that multimedia developers are artists in their own right, this book would never have been published.

ABOUT THE AUTHOR

Phil got his start with PCs while working on a political science degree at Syracuse University. His only application of computing to politics was an internship spent as director of data processing for an unsuccessful mayoral campaign. While it was fun earning academic credit for trying to take city hall, he decided that politics was just too messy to seriously pursue. His first job was as technical support manager for Show Partner, a popular on-screen presentation package. Since leaving that position in 1988, Phil has done freelance programming on demos for Lotus, Computer Associates, Adobe Systems, and Intel.

Currently, Phil is a freelance multimedia developer based in London, England. You can reach him on Compuserve 76470,233.

PREFACE

Walkthroughs & Flybys CD is a book about a collection of art. Now you've all seen flashy demos, but how much do you really know about what it takes to make one? Read on and you'll discover the tricks, tips, and techniques that separate the hobbyists from the pros. We present the stories behind the pixels and sounds, hoping for nothing more than to inspire you the reader and try to make your next foray into multimedia that much more challenging.

About six years ago I first became involved with people who produced animated computer graphics for a living. The company I was working for at the time had introduced a new presentation package called Show Partner. Every support call I took offered a different perspective on the types of problems these commercial artists faced. Since it seemed to be such an interesting business, I decided to quit my technical support job and leap in with both feet.

Since there is no better way to get ideas than to examine the work of others, I embarked on a course of collecting demos who I found to be of interest and establishing contact with those who created them. Over the years my contacts grew, as did the collection of demos that I accumulated. Through the CompuServe Information Network, ideas and techniques were shared with an openness that would surprise many professionals in today's highly competitive software business.

The story behind this book really starts in the summer of 1991 when my company was approached by Nimbus Information Systems to produce a demonstration CD for free distribution. The people at Nimbus were so impressed with our graphics that they agreed to make us a CD for free and give us 500 copies, as long as they could distribute 500 copies as well. Knowing that we could only come up with around 50MB of material that was good enough to consider distributing, we put out the word on CompuServe for other artists to send in contributions. The response really floored us, and before we knew where we were, we had a 540MB dataset that blew the doors off anything else available at the time. Of all the contributors to this project none gave a more hearty endorsement, or more graphics, than Autodesk Multimedia Division.

At about the same time one of my CompuServe pen pals, Mitch Waite, had just taken delivery of his first Sound Blaster Multimedia Upgrade kit. Mitch liked our CD so much that we decided to produce a new product with the latest demos available; the result of which you hold in your hands.

This book was written for the sole purpose of establishing a collection of PC-based art. Just as no museum is complete without a guidebook, this mass of demos and 3D animations is no different. Enjoy the book and remember that no artist can live in a vacuum. It is only through the sharing of techniques that each person's horizons are broadened.

Phil Shatz
Summer 1993
CompuServe 76470,233

ABOUT THIS BOOK

The first chapter serves as an introduction to the book while the second describes the layout of the CD. The next three chapters each deal with a different category of demonstration material. In Chapter 3 you'll read about presentations designed specifically to be used in conjunction with the Sound Blaster. Chapter 4 is devoted to the world of Autodesk 3D Studio and the fantastic animations that have been created using it. Finally, Chapter 5 focuses on demos created with GRASP but also gives cursory examination to work created with Deluxe Paint Animation and Domark's Virtual Reality Toolkit.

Dear Reader,

While racing through the exhibits at a CD-ROM conference, I ran into the Nimbus booth, a CD-duplicating service, and took home "Hot Stuff," a free demo disc. I spilled open my bag o' treats from the show, fired up my MPC machine (486/66 with Sound Blaster and CD-ROM drive) and shoved the Hot Stuff disc in the player. I began looking for some kind of program to start. There was no program. Instead there was a tiny batch file called SBGO.BAT.

I typed SBGO.BAT, which ran a program called BIGDEMO. It was the most amazing collection of 3D movies and synched music I had ever seen or heard on a PC. Beautiful digital movies made with Autodesk's 3D Studio twirled objects with fluid motion while digitized music recorded in Sound Blaster VOC format pounded through me in perfect time. It wasn't just the images and sounds that kept me spellbound, but the incredible creativity of the content. Magical camera viewpoints rocketed over fractal mountains, logos gyrated more gracefully than TV network IDs, cars morphed into animals, billiard balls melted into puddles, glass shattered into a million facets, trucks grew robot legs and walked over cars.

I found the CD-ROM was arranged like a large 600MB hard disk, complete with cryptic directories and subdirectories. Inside these I found a treasure chest of Autodesk flick movies, international demos, GRASP multimedia demos, utilities, sound effects, recorded music, fractal zooms, machine simulations, chess matches, medical exams, and much more. The Finnish demos were the most wild yet — all hard coded in assembly language and squeezing things out of a PC I hadn't thought possible.

While the CD-ROM's content was astounding, its complex directory structure made it time consuming and difficult to navigate. And there was no information on how these demos and movies were made. Suddenly a light bulb went on over my head…this CD would be great with a good explanatory book and an improved menuing system. I contacted the CD-ROM's author, Phil Shatz, on Compuserve to share my idea. And here it is, *Walkthroughs and Flybys CD*.

We hope you enjoy the book. We're always looking for demos and animations for the next edition of *W&F*, so see the back of the book for submission info. And for a color catalog, just fill out and send in the Satisfaction Report Card at the back of the book. You can reach me on CIS as 75146,3515, MCI mail as mwaite, and usenet as mitch@well.sf.ca.us.

Sincerely,

Mitchell Waite

Mitchell Waite

WAITE
GROUP
PRESS™

WALKTHROUGHS & FLYBYS CD

TABLE OF CONTENTS

CONTENTS

CONVENTIONS

The spelling of the word "disk" refers to a standard magnetic floppy while "disc" refers to a CD-ROM.

The terms "flic" and "movie" both mean animations stored in the Autodesk FLI or FLC format.

READ THIS PAGE BEFORE USING THE CD

In the event that you are eager to get started immediately, please take a moment to read the important information on this page.

- Detailed installation instructions can be found in Chapter 2.

- The Installation program, INSTALL.EXE, will create a \WF subdirectory on your hard disk into which around 80k of files will be copied. These files make up the menu system that loads when you execute the file WF.BAT. WF.BAT is generated during installation, not copied from the CD, and will be placed in the root of your hard disk.

- Be sure to reboot your computer after running INSTALL.EXE.

- While most demos run off the CD, certain demos need to be loaded from the hard disk as they require much faster disk access times than the CD provides. Each time you choose one of these demos, the menu system will ask you onto which drive you wish to copy these files. The menu system will not delete files from the \WFTEMP subdirectory. That you have to do yourself.

- The **Make a Boot Disk** option available from the main menu will copy 11MB of the most memory intensive Sound Blaster demos to your hard disk before formatting a bootable system disk. Another way to do this is to copy all the demos to the hard disk at once.

- You will not need to use the **Make Boot Disk** option, if your system has more than 600K of free RAM after loading DOS and also has Expanded Memory available. In the event that any of the Sound Blaster demos crash on your system, use the **Make Boot Disk** option.

- The **Make a Boot Disk** option uses the DOS FORMAT.COM program to format the boot disk. If this DOS program is named anything other than FORMAT.COM the **Make a Boot Disk** option will not work. Please rename the file to FORMAT.COM.

- If you find you are having problems running a demo, read the troubleshooting tips found in Appendix D.

CHAPTER

A NEW INDUSTRY

FOR NEW ARTISTS

There is no area of computing that allows more freedom of expression than multimedia software development. It is now possible to create whatever the mind can imagine in the virtual world of the PC. However, fulfilling fantasies doesn't always come easy. Although there may be a wealth of user friendly software available, most companies still prefer to hire specialists to produce multimedia for them rather than investing the resources to develop that capability in-house. These experts and their creations are the focus of this book.

The *Walkthroughs & Flybys CD* contains over 500MB of the best graphics ever produced for the PC. As you can see from the illustration in Figure 1-1, the CD we've compiled contains over 375 floppy disks worth of data. The material ranges from painfully serious medical applications to mind-bending and foot-stomping Sound Blaster demos. While the overwhelming majority of disc space is given to full motion animations created with Autodesk 3D Studio, we also give extensive coverage to demos made with GRASP, a popular DOS-based program that has been available for several years now. You'll also be introduced to Europe's leading demo groups that specialize in producing high-speed animations with sound in custom-coded assembly language. As we lead you through the various categories of multimedia, we will share what we think is special and unique about each demo. In some cases, you will be given background information on the

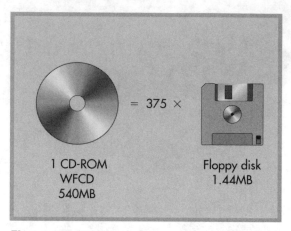

Figure 1-1 375 floppy disks would be required to hold the *Walkthroughs & Flybys CD* collection

artist and be taught how they accomplish their incredible effects. Our goal is to inspire, excite, and stimulate ideas as we lead you on a journey through what is possible today on the PC with graphics and sound.

PROMOTING THE ARTISTS

Because the majority of the contributing artists to *Walkthroughs & Flybys CD* are occupied full time with the production of PC graphics, becoming known is particularly important to their success. Given that this type of service bureau is so new, often the artists must sell the concept of using multimedia in order to sell themselves. Fortunately, provided that the quality of their work is good and its exposure to the public is high, the chances for a creative and disciplined artist to make big money are rather favorable.

The biggest problem for these artists is that so many demos aren't seen. Replicating floppy disks is expensive and, generally, these applications are too big to be beamed around the world over the phone lines with modems. Until now, no one has taken advantage of the awesome capacity, light weight, and inexpensive replication costs of CD-ROM in order to distribute a collection of the best demos. In planning this book, quality was our only criterion for inclusion and our focus was always on the artist responsible. With *Walkthroughs & Flybys CD*, we have tried to present first a brief overview of the software technology before showing it in action. We offer new ideas for how to use multimedia to your advantage by presenting a smorgasbord of prior successes.

The Issue of Copyright: These works of art are **not** in the public domain. Each piece has been contributed to *Walkthroughs & Flybys CD* on the condition that the artist is credited with his or her work and that the copyright remains fully and totally with him. The vast majority of contributing artists are full-time professionals in the demo business for whom the production of computer art is their livelihood. You, as the purchaser of this book, are **not** free to use any of the graphics or sounds on the accompanying disc in your own projects without the permission of the contributing artist. If you enjoy a particular person's style and it is convenient for you to contact them, please do. Putting admirers and potential clients in touch with experts in the field is one of the main objectives of *Walkthroughs & Flybys CD*.

CONTACTING THE ARTISTS

As we present the work of various artists in the chapters that follow, their names and the names of their companies or groups will be provided in the description. If you want to contact the creators directly, their addresses, phone, fax, and CompuServe account numbers are listed in Appendix A, *Contributor Listings*. If you want to find out who created a particular animation that isn't described in the text. See Appendix D for a full listing of the disc contents.

As you read through this book, please remember that it isn't a guide to making demos but rather a collection of the best ones. There are already a great many books available about how to use the various tools of the demo trade, but what has been lacking is a single source of the best work done to date. Through the awesome capacity of CD-ROM, we can bring hundreds of megabytes of this material to you in a compact, inexpensive, and hopefully organized manner. Prepare yourself for a ride into the virtual world of PC demos.

CHAPTER 2

LAYOUT OF THE CD

540MB is a large amount of data to find one's way around. To make navigating through this collection of multimedia easier, we've devoted this chapter to describing the contents of the CD in a general way. There are three main categories of material into which the chapters of the book and the directories of the disc have been divided.

The first of these categories comprises demos that integrate graphics and sound. Because of the tremendous demands that these types of programs make upon the resources of the PC, they are, for the most part, coded in custom assembly language rather than utilizing off-the-shelf presentation packages.

The second category of material includes animations in the flic format that have been created with Autodesk 3D Studio. This exciting program is used to create the journeys into virtual worlds that inspired the title of this book.

The third category, while focused on demos created with GRASP, also covers computer art produced with tools such as Deluxe Paint Animation and Domark's Virtual Reality Toolkit, as well as a proprietary system.

THE DIRECTORY STRUCTURE

Aside from the three main directories of demos, a fourth directory contains various utilities and programs. The four directories branching from the root of the CD are as follows:

9

- ⊛ \SBDEMOS   Coded specifically for the Sound Blaster

- ⊛ \FLIC   Autodesk flics made with 3D Studio or Animator

- ⊛ \DEMOS   Other demos of all types

- ⊛ \PROGRAMS   Various tools and utilities

Beneath each of these root level directories, you will find other subdirectories. In \SBDEMOS and \DEMOS, each team of artists has been given its own directory or branch of subdirectories to keep its files separate. For example, all of the Sound Blaster demos by the Future Crew are located in a directory called \SBDEMOS\FUTURE_C.

Flics are animations stored in Autodesk's differential file format for bitmaps. Because flic animations are completely contained in a single file, there was no need to separate them by artist. Instead, we created two directories for the two variations of the flic format. The \FLICS\FLI directory contains animations in the FLI format introduced with Autodesk Animator. All of these files are in the standard VGA 320x200x256 color format. The directory \FLICS\FLC contains animations in the newer FLC format. Although FLC files can be of variable resolutions, you will find that the majority of these files are 640x480x256 colors. Animations demonstrating the use of 3D Studio's IPAS external processes have been given their own directory, \FLIC\IPAS, to keep them separate from the others.

The top-level directory, \PROGRAMS, contains the various executable files needed to play animations or display pictures. The files for the navigation menu system are also located in this subdirectory. Users of the popular Norton Change Directory program, NCD.EXE, will find that we have included a TREEINFO.NCD file in the root directory to ease manual navigation of the hierarchy of the CD.

THE AUTOMENU NAVIGATION SYSTEM

The Automenu system from Magee Enterprises was used to create the interface for the *Walkthroughs & Flybys CD*. By using this popular and flexible system, you can build a comprehensive interface for a vast number of disparate programs very quickly. In a nutshell, this system works by writing a DOS batch file and then terminating whenever a selection is made from one of the menus. After Automenu terminates, the newly written batch file executes, carrying out the commands corresponding with your selection. When the batch file is finished, Automenu is reloaded.

Automenu's ability to completely unload itself makes it a perfect menu development system for any CD-ROM full of memory-hungry demos. But there is a catch to using Automenu to create a menu system for a CD-ROM. Because it is not possible to create files on a read-only device such as a CD-ROM, the menu system must first be installed onto your hard disk.

Installing the Automenu Navigation Menu System

To get started, switch to the drive containing the CD and execute the file INSTALL.EXE, which you will find in the root directory of the *Walkthroughs & Flybys CD*. If you receive an error message saying that your "DOS environment" is full, see Appendix B, *Troubleshooting,* for instructions on how to increase the size of this area. At the first install prompt (Figure 2-1), choose a drive letter onto which you would like to install the menu system. Because only about 70K is needed, don't worry about losing too much of your precious hard disk space. Press the key corresponding to the drive letter onto which you want to install the menu system. Valid drive letters accepted at this prompt are C:\ through G:\. If you want to abort the installation for any reason, press any key other than Ⓒ through Ⓖ at this screen.

The second screen of INSTALL.EXE displays the source and target drives for the installation as well as giving you another chance to abort gracefully. If you press Ⓨ at this prompt, a \WF directory will be created on the target drive and the menu system will be copied into it. You will see that the progress of the installation is displayed on the screen as the files are copied. After the menu system has been copied, INSTALL.EXE will generate a WF.BAT file in both the root and \WF directories. You can get started by entering WF at the DOS prompt.

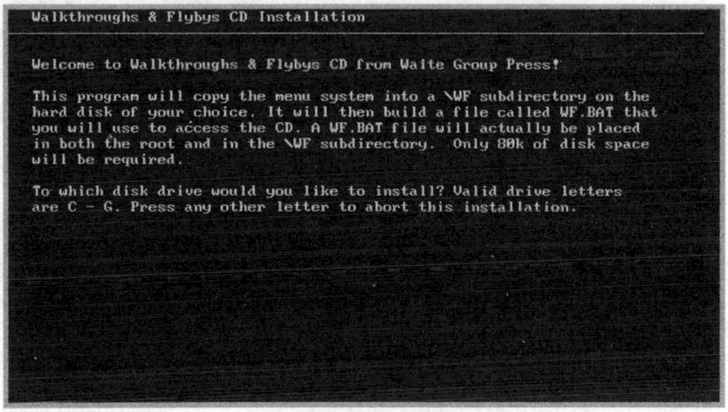

```
Walkthroughs & Flybys CD Installation

Welcome to Walkthroughs & Flybys CD from Walte Group Press!

This program will copy the menu system into a \WF subdirectory on the
hard disk of your choice. It will then build a file called WF.BAT that
you will use to access the CD. A WF.BAT file will actually be placed
in both the root and in the \WF subdirectory.  Only 80k of disk space
will be required.

To which disk drive would you like to install? Valid drive letters
are C - G. Press any other letter to abort this installation.
```

Figure 2-1 The initial screen of INSTALL.EXE

Using the Menu System

From this single menu, over 200 different demos and animations are just a few keypresses away. If you want to see demos for the Sound Blaster, press (ENTER) with the first option highlighted. For Autodesk flic animations, choose the second. All demos created with GRASP are accessed under the third choice, and the fourth is left for demos in all other categories. Selecting option five loads a submenu from which you can obtain general information about this book and the CD. The sixth option contains a procedure to generate a bootable floppy disk allowing you to run even the most memory intensive demos without altering your system configuration.

As seen in Figure 2-2, the Automenu system is an absolute cinch to use, allowing you to choose options in any of three ways. The easiest is to move the highlighted selection bar up and down with the mouse, pressing either mouse button to make your selection. The menu bar can also be moved with the arrow keys and the selection made by pressing the (ENTER) key. You can also press the key corresponding to the number of your selection. When the selection bar passes over an item, a message at the bottom of the screen describes that option. Although each submenu contains an option to return to its parent, only this top-level menu contains an option allowing you to quit to DOS. The menu system also functions as a screen saver that will be activated after 10 minutes of inactivity. If you are interested in finding out more information about Automenu, press (H) for help and (P) for Program Information.

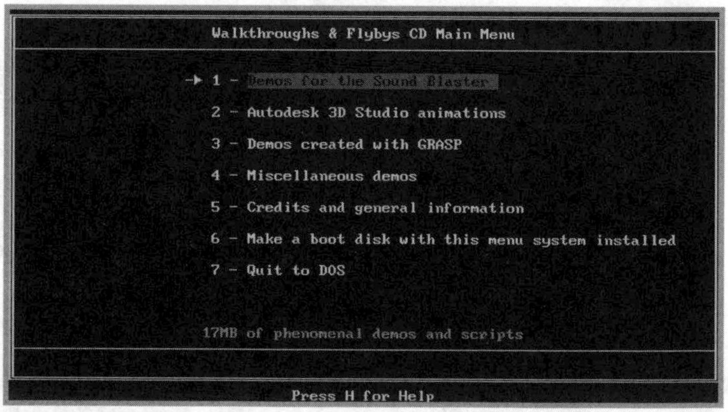

Figure 2-2 The *Walkthroughs & Flybys CD* Main Menu

Now that you have gotten the hang of the menu system, let's jump right into the Sound Blaster demos, which contain some of the most exciting demonstration material ever created on PCs! If your system isn't equipped with a Sound Blaster or compatible audio card such as the Media Vision Pro Audio Spectrum, you will probably want to skip to Chapter 4, *The Autodesk World of 3-D Movies*, where Autodesk flics are covered.

THE CONTENTS OF THE DISC

Table 2-1 lists the entire contents of *Walkthroughs & Flybys CD*. To preserve space we have omitted listing each of the 139 animation files in the Autodesk flic format.

TABLE 2-1 THE CONTENTS OF THE DISC

CHAPTER 3 SOUND BLASTER DEMOS
Total size of category: 47MB

Creator or Team	Core File	Demo Title	Size(K)	WF Address
Cascada	CRONOLOG.EXE	Cronologia	474	SBDEMOS\CASCADA
Future Crew Productions	FISHTRO.EXE	Fishtro	531	SBDEMOS\FUTURE_C
Future Crew Productions	PANIC.EXE	Panic	1693	SBDEMOS\FUTURE_C
Future Crew Productions	SCREAM_T.ZIP	Scream Tracker	269	SBDEMOS\FUTURE_C
Future Crew Productions	MENTAL_S.ZIP	Mental Surgery	245	SBDEMOS\FUTURE_C
Future Crew Productions	THEPARTY.EXE	The Party	245	SBDEMOS\FUTURE_C
Future Crew Productions	UNREAL.EXE	UNREAL	2310	SBDEMOS\FUTURE_C
Future Crew Productions	WFDEMO.EXE	Walkthroughs & Flybys	269	SBDEMOS\FUTURE_C
White & Boese	BIGDEMO.SB	The BIGDEMO	11000*	SBDEMOS\BIGDEMO
Starcom CDROM	STARCOM.SB	Fractal Zoom	22866**	SBDEMOS\STARCOM
Triton	CRYSTAL.EXE	Crystal Dream	1490	SBDEMOS\TRITON
Ultraforce	VECTDEMO.EXE	VECTDEMO	293	SBDEMOS\ULTRA_F
Ultraforce	DENTRO.COM	Dentro	365	SBDEMOS\ULTRA_F
ORIGIN Systems	WING2.EXE	Wing Commander II Demo	3500	SBDEMOS\ORIGIN
Witan	FACTS.EXE	Facts of Life	2204	SBDEMOS\WITAN

* Size figure is just digitized audio

** Size figure includes both audio and graphics

(table continues)

CHAPTER 4: THE AUTODESK WORLD OF 3-D MOVIES
Total size of category: 360MB

Category	Number of Files	Total Size (K)
Standard VGA FLIs	93	265642
SuperVGA FLCs	17	84069
FLI files created with IPAS	29	10505

CHAPTER 5: DEMOS FOR THE PC
Total size of category: 141MB

Creator or Team	Core File	Demo Title	Size(K)	WF Address
ASDI	PIONEER.EXE	Pioneer Home Theatre Demo	2140	DEMOS\ASDI
Carr Charles	3DHOUSE.BAT	Domarks Virtual Reality Studio	148	DEMOS\CARR
Digital Image Ltd	HSEGOLD.EXE	HSE Logo made with Topaz	3421	DEMOS\DIGIT_I
Digital Image Ltd	KIDZ640.EXE	Rotoscoped Video with Topaz	2200	DEMOS\DIGIT_I
Digital Image Ltd	POUND640.EXE	Rotating 3D Pound Sign	3556	DEMOS\DIGIT_I
Digital Image Ltd	TAP.EXE	A Water Tap	891	DEMOS\DIGIT_I
Enlighten	ACPDEMO.EXE	CA ACCPAC Plus Demo	2252	DEMOS\ENLIGHTE
Enlighten	CBVDEMO.EXE	CA CobolVision Demo	2151	DEMOS\ENLIGHTE
Enlighten	CLIPDEMO.EXE	CA Clipper Demo	2361	DEMOS\ENLIGHTE
Enlighten	DBFDEMO.EXE	CA dbFast Demo	2592	DEMOS\ENLIGHTE
Enlighten	ENLCARD.EXE	What to do with Christmas Fruitcake	2546	DEMOS\ENLIGHTE
Enlighten	READEMO.EXE	CA Realizer Demo	2184	DEMOS\ENLIGHTE
Enlighten	SCDEMO.EXE	CA SuperCalc Demo	2375	DEMOS\ENLIGHTE
Enlighten	SPCEVENT.EXE	Harvard Graphics Event on a Disk	1690	DEMOS\ENLIGHTE
Enlighten	TXTDEMO.EXE	CA Textor Demo	1894	DEMOS\ENLIGHTE
FLIX Productions	AWORDS.EXE	Animated Words learning program for kids	1400	DEMOS\FLIX
Griffin Studios	PUZZLE.EXE	Puzzled by Promotion	1287	DEMOS\GRIFFIN
Houston Graphics	SK2DEMO.EXE	Borland Sidekick 2 Demo	580	DEMOS\HOUSTON
Houston Graphics	SL25DEMO.EXE	Everex SL25 demo	1878	DEMOS\HOUSTON
Houston Graphics	XMASCARD.EXE	Holiday Greeting	1493	DEMOS\HOUSTON
IMS	CU.EXE	Commercial Union Demo	1165	DEMOS\IMS\COMMERC
IMS	DEMO.EXE	IIT Xtra Drive demo	1166	DEMOS\IMS\IIT_XD
IMS	IIT.EXE	IIT Math Coprocessor demo	1166	DEMOS\IMS\IIT_MATH
IMS	OAG.EXE	Offical Airlines Guide demo	702	DEMOS\IMS\OAG
IMS	QUANTUM.EXE	Thomas Cook's Quantum Demo	410	DEMOS\IMS\THOMAS_C

(table continues)

Creator or Team	Core File	Demo Title	Size(K)	WF Address
IMS	VICTOR1.EXE	Victor - A Company with a History	7035	DEMOS\IMS\VICTOR
IMS	VLSAMPLE.EXE	Videologic Product Sampler	1719	DEMOS\IMS\VIDEOLOG
IMS	START.EXE	Xerox Engineering Systems	11320	DEMOS\IMS\XEROX
Marketing Systems	MARKETSY.EXE	Marketing Systems Demo	1931	DEMOS\MARKETSY
Marketing Systems	MKTSY2.EXE	Marketing Systems & Chromagraphics	1493	DEMOS\MARKETSY
Medical Multimedia	DEMOBACK.EXE	Patient's Guide to Lower Back Pain	2095	DEMOS\MEDICALM
Medical Multimedia	ROUNDS.EXE	Montana Rounds Thumb Problems	847	DEMOS\MEDICALM
Multimedia Music Co.	Audio track 1	Playing Graphics with CD Audio	*	Audio track 1
Pulver Bill	WINE.EXE	Raytraced Animation with Big D	810	DEMOS\PULVER
Screen Artists Ltd	92COL.BAT	The ICL 92 Collection	35930	DEMOS\SARTISTS
Screen Artists Ltd	PSDEMO.EXE	ICL People Working Together demo	6234	DEMOS\SARTISTS
Screen Artists Ltd	T2000.EXE	Toshiba T2000 Demo	2703	DEMOS\SARTISTS
Shaddock Phil	DEMOFLUK.EXE	Demo for John Fluke Co.	3438	DEMOS\SHADDOCK
Silver Tongue	PEAPOD.EXE	Peapod Kiosk Demo Disk	2956	DEMOS\SILVER_T\VGA
Silver Tongue	PEAPOD.EXE	Peapod Kiosk Application	6028	DEMOS\SILVER_T\SVGA
Systemax	MAXDEMO.EXE	Maximizer for Windows Demo	2722	DEMOS\SYSTEMAX
Systemax	DNEWS002.EXE	DiscNews Volume 2	1290	DEMOS\SYSTEMAX
Systemax	GREET91.EXE	Holiday Disc Greeting	662	DEMOS\SYSTEMAX
Systemax	WPDEMO.EXE	LaserMaster WinPrint Demo	2563	DEMOS\SYSTEMAX
The Artwork Exchange	DEMO1.BAT	Wormville	3279	DEMOS\NESSLING
The Artwork Exchange	DEMO2.BAT	Watch This Space	2752	DEMOS\NESSLING

* While this audio track does technically occupy more than 50MB of space on the disc
it has not been included in the size figures above.

CHAPTER 3

SOUND BLASTER

DEMOS

It's only in the last couple of years that PCs have advanced to the point where demonstrations can be accompanied by sound. Because the PC speaker really makes horrible sounds, extra hardware is needed if you want to hear anything worth listening to. The most common, affordable, and standard sound card for the PC is the Sound Blaster from Creative Labs Inc. This device has opened the doorway to multimedia computing by giving software developers an easy way to off-load the processing requirements of generating audio from the CPU to a coprocessor. In this chapter, we will look at demos written specifically for the Sound Blaster.

THE BIGDEMO

Niko Boese, Peter White & Phil Shatz

11MB of audio
180MB of graphics
Requires 520K free RAM
Keys: (CTRL)-(END) to quit

Figure 3-1 Screen shot of the BIGDEMO opening

To introduce your journey through *Walkthroughs & Flybys CD* we've chosen a half hour long odyssey of animations set to music (Figure 3-1). Niko Boese composed the music and converted it to Sound Blaster format while Peter White and Phil Shatz did the MMPLAY script programming. We'll discuss MMPLAY and the Sound Blaster in more depth after we have you up and running.

To start the BIGDEMO all you have to do is load the menu system and make the following selections:

```
The BIGDEMO requires 520k of free memory to run through to completion
without error. This PC currently has 542k free.

The Sound Blaster driver files from Creative Labs have been found!

If you have a Sound Blaster Pro, make sure all your volume levels are
high enough. Sound Blaster 16 ASP users should choose option 2.

Choose either 1 Run this MMPLAY script with the drivers that have
               been found on your PC,

            2 Install a set of drivers from the CD into your C:\WF
               directory. Your SOUND environment variable will be set
               to point to these files rather than your existing drivers.
               Choosing this setting will alter your configuration
               until you reboot,

            3 Abort and return to the menu system.

Press either 1,2 or 3
```

Figure 3-2 BIGDEMO option screen

**Demos for the Sound Blaster,
MMPLAY Scripts Menu** and
The BIGDEMO by Peter White, Niko Boese & Phil Shatz.

If the Sound Blaster driver files exist and are correctly installed, you will be presented with the screen shown in Figure 3-2. Choose the first option to run the BIGDEMO with your drivers.

You are also able to choose the **Install a set of drivers from the CD** option that will let you run the BIGDEMO even if your Sound Blaster is incorrectly installed. If you are using a 100% compatible card, such as the Media Vision Pro Audio Spectrum, then installation of the drivers from the CD will begin without asking you first. Here's what the installation routine does:

- Creates a subdirectory called \WF\DRV and places the required CT-VOICE.DRV file into it

- Creates a DOS environment variable called SOUND that will point to \WF

- Prompts you for the Interrupt and I/O address of your Sound Blaster from which the required BLASTER environment variable is created

If you would like the BIGDEMO to play only once before returning to the menu system, press the Ⓨ key at the final prompt. If you press Ⓝ, then the BIGDEMO will play forever.

The BIGDEMO leads off with a Waite Group Press logo flying in from behind the camera to a burst of music. If you don't hear anything, check your cables and volume levels before referring to Appendix B for troubleshooting information.

Note: To quit from the BIGDEMO press CTRL-END.

Short of rebooting your computer, there is only one way to quit MMPLAY scripts. Hold down the CTRL key and press END. The END key is the same as the ① key on the numeric keypad. After a couple of seconds you will be returned to the menu. There are no other keys active during the BIGDEMO other than CTRL-END.

The graphics you see were created for the most part with Autodesk 3D Studio by dozens of animators in a number of different countries. While many of these files were sent in by their creators, a large amount of the material was contributed en masse by Autodesk Corporation. To simplify the presentation of this tour, rather than describe every animation as it appears in the sequence, only certain ones will be mentioned. In Chapter 4, *The Autodesk World of 3-D Movies*, we take a closer look at the product 3D Studio, and the marvelous animations that have been created with it.

BIGDEMO Tour Highlights

We will present the work of various artists in turn over the next half an hour. All of the flics described below are located in the directory \FLIC\FLI of the disc from which they are accessed by MMPLAY. These files are in the standard Autodesk Animator 1.0 format, which is 320x200 resolution with 256 colors.

Figure 3-3

WF1.FLI (See Figure 3-3.) The human figure was originally created with Mannequin software from HumanCAD before being imported into 3D Studio. The walking motion was created by Phil Shatz in 3D Studio Release 1.0. The dragon on the right was created by Michael Mulholland.

Figure 3-4

A3DSLOGO.FLI (See Figure 3-4.) An animated 3D Studio logo appears right after the race cars. Notice the way that the marble textured hemispheres change into donuts while shadows race across the plane. When 3D objects transform themselves into new shapes like this, we call the process morphing.

Figure 3-5

DOLPHIN.FLI (See Figure 3-5.) Originally created by Simon Browne at 640x480 resolution, this flic was reduced to 320x200 during the process of creating the BIGDEMO. You will find the original file in the \FLIC\FLC directory. Simon's work is given a thorough examination in the section "In the Style of MC Escher" that you will find in Chapter 4.

Figure 3-6

INVOKE.FLI (See Figure 3-6.) Gary Yost created this human figure with a beta copy of Mannequin before importing the file into 3D Studio. This animation of a kneeling chrome woman moving her arms has to be one of the most widespread flic files ever. Notice how perfect the shadow is and the way that the ball morphs into a sphere.

Figure 3-7

SPURT.FLI (See Figure 3-7.) This eruption of purple and blue liquid is one of a number of files demonstrating the power of the 3D Studio IPAS interface for external processes. You will find over 30 different animations demonstrating this amazing capablity in the \FLIC\IPAS directory.

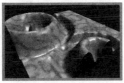

Figure 3-8

DROPIT2.FLI (See Figure 3-8.) An orange and white marble plane mutates into various shapes that move around four points of a square and then flatten out into a plane again. The plane then begins to undulate like a 3-D sine wave. This sequence was created with Renderman, but this effect should now be possible with 3D Studio Release 2.0 thanks to its IPAS interface. If you are interested in this type of morphing animation, be sure to view the IPAS examples described in Chapter 4, *The Autodesk World of 3 D Movies*.

Figure 3-9

BOOKSPIN.FLI (See Figure 3-9.) This is a flic file of a book that comes out of the distance and grows larger before opening. It was created by Marcus Morgan during his employment at Autodesk UK Ltd. Note how the light glints off the cover of the book as it spins into view. The effect of the turning pages demonstrates how the axis around which an object rotates can be easily moved. The smoothness with which the pages gently curl reveal the power of 3D Studio's ability to morph between objects.

Figure 3-10

VENUS.FLI (See Figure 3-10.) This rotating human torso is clearly recognizable as Michelangelo's Venus de Milo. The mesh (3-D wireframe model) for this object was created on a Macintosh using a 3-D digitizing device. It was then imported into 3D Studio as a DXF file by Gary Yost.

Figure 3-11

BRIDGEFLY.FLI (See Figure 3-11.) This illustrates an outstanding example of flight simulation. There are quite a few interesting things in this flic of a helicopter circling around a bridge. Notice how effectively adding some fog reinforces the illusion of distance and speed. In 3D Studio creating this type of atmospheric effect is as easy as selecting a single option button!

The massive size of the bridge and the nature of its shape lend itself perfectly to this type of fly-through. Also be sure to notice how the illusion of motion blur is created by the rotor of the helicopter slowly spinning within a translucent circle.

Figure 3-12

NEWTONLO.FLI (See Figure 3-12.) Marcus Morgan created this model of a Newton's Cradle while he was with Autodesk UK Ltd. While the motion is quite realistic, the lack of automatic reflection mapping in 3D Studio Release 1.0 is a definite detraction. If this file were rendered again in Release 2.0, you would see the reflection of the vertical bars of the cradle mapped onto the suspended balls with perfect accuracy.

Figure 3-13

FISH_1.FLI - FISH_5.FLI (See Figure 3-13.) This five file, 10MB series of flics were originally created by Autodesk and the Yost Group for part of a video that shipped with every copy of Animator. The purpose of this video was not so much to show off the capabilities of the program but to inspire the users of the product. Judging by the numbers of people that have commented on CompuServe that the video was their major source for new ideas, it was very successful in this regard. The original sequence was broken up into smaller FLI files and then put to music by Creative Labs Inc., the Sound Blaster people. You'll notice that the animation stops completely when the voice file for one of the fish is loaded. If the BIGDEMO was playing from a hard disk, the faster seek time would cause that delay to be almost unnoticeable.

Figure 3-14

VIV_PRE.FLI (SeeFigure 3-14.) This shows the imaginary Virtual Image Spaceship spinning into view while being accompanied by a lovely little piece of Niko Boese's music. This remarkable 11.5MB animation by Adam Maitland demonstrates the power of using AutoCAD and 3D Studio together to create realistic visualizations of architectural models. Essentially, the plans for the spaceship were created in AutoCAD and then imported into 3D Studio via the DXF format. Toward the end of this flic you will notice an animating 3-D Perpetual Motion machine hanging on the wall. As it is illiustrated here, mapping a flic onto an object is real easy in 3D Studio.

Figure 3-15

PERPETUA.FLI (See Figure 3-15.) This is the second of the two incredible animations created by Adam Maitland that are included in *Walkthroughs & Flybys CD*. See the detailed analysis of this FLI file in the next chapter.

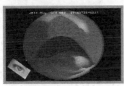

Figure 3-16

3DEYE.FLI (See Figure 3-16.) Jeff Alu created this stereoscopic flic. The images composing this animation were separated into their red and blue components with PICLAB. If you wear red and blue anaglyphic glasses when you watch this flic it will appear in 3-D.

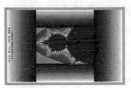

Figure 3-17

FRACZOOM.FLI (See Figure 3-17.) This ride into the depths of the Mandelbrot set was created by Jeff Alu with FRACTINT, a very popular program that works like a fractal microscope. Since fractals are essentially mathematical formulas that exhibit chaotic behavior, plotting their values produces marvelous patterns. If you like this sequence, be sure to run the **Starcom Fractal Zoom** from the **MMPLAY Scripts Menu** descriptive text of which follows in the next section. (To learn more about fractals and using FRACTINT, see *Fractal Creations* by Wegner & Peterson, The Waite Group Press, 1992, 430 pages, $34.95.)

Figure 3-18

CYCART_1.FLI (See Figure 3-18.) This flic was created by Rob Stien III of Anigraf/x. As one of the lead animators with Trilobyte, Rob has worked on several popular game titles including the recently released 7th Guest from Virgin Games. For a closer look at work from this artist, see the section "Creating the Haunting and Supernatural" in Chapter 4, *The Autodesk World of 3-D Movies*.

Figure 3-19

FLIGHT.FLI (See Figure 3-19.) The intensity of the colors used in this flic help it to stand out. Unlike most of the animations in this format, different sections of this file have different color palettes. The 3D Studio models used to create the airplanes in this animation are commercially available from Technical Designs. They also have a library of 3-D People that are quite handy for all sorts of projects.

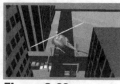

Figure 3-20

CHOPCITY.FLI (See Figure 3-20.) This is a nice animation of a chopper flying through a city, which unfortunately plays a bit slowly from CD-ROM. This is because the degree of change from frame to frame of the animation is much higher than the CD-ROM can provide. You see, the Autodesk flic format achieves its fast frame rate by playing back just the differences between pictures so that in sequences with a great degree of change, such as this one, the I/O bottleneck becomes quite acute.

MMPLAY — A Simple but Effective Sequencing Tool

As you have just seen, the MMPLAY scripting language distributed with the Sound Blaster can be a very powerful tool in the hands of the skilled and patient. This program works by executing a simple script containing commands for playing either sequenced or digitized sounds simultaneously with displaying Autodesk Animator flic files. If you like to do your computing at the command line, MMPLAY may be just the utility for you. There is no user interface to like or dislike with MMPLAY. Just write a script and feed it to this single executable file. Spartan as the tool may be, it is the simplest and most effective way to sequence FLI files with sound. To give you a feel for what it's like to build an MMPLAY script, we've provided a listing of the first 10 minutes of the BIGDEMO.SB script file. The text in the right-hand column lists comments that have been added to make the script easier to follow.

LISTING 3-1 THE BIGDEMO MMPLAY SCRIPT

```
.vout mus2targ                  Play digitized sound file
.aplay1 \flic\fli\wf1           Play animation WF1.FLI once
.aplay1 \flic\fli\cars_big      Play CARS_BIG.FLI once
.delay 75                       wait for .75 second
.stop v                         stop the VOC file

.vout mus4targ                  Play digitized sound file
.aplay1 \flic\fli\a3dsdemo      Play animation
.aplay1 \flic\fli\3dslogo       Play animation
.aplay1 \flic\fli\to21          Display Simon's title slide
.delay 300                      Wait for 3 seconds
.aplay1 \flic\fli\head1
.aplay1 \flic\fli\dolphin
.aplay1 \flic\fli\room
.aplay1 \flic\fli\room
.sync V0                        Set sync point so FISH.FLI
```

```
.aplay \flic\fli\fish                    repeats till music ends

.vout mus3targ
.aplay1 \flic\fli\to17
.delay 300
.aplay1 \flic\fli\invoke
.aplay1 \flic\ipas\IPASFWRK              Begin playing IPAS animations
.aplay1 \flic\ipas\STRETCH
.aplay1 \flic\ipas\mwave
.aplay1 \flic\ipas\mwave_1
.aplay1 \flic\ipas\flare
.aplay1 \flic\ipas\flare
.aplay1 \flic\ipas\glow
.aplay1 \flic\ipas\spurt
.aplay1 \flic\ipas\explod_5
.aplay1 \flic\ipas\EXPLODE2
.aplay1 \flic\ipas\SNOW
.sync V0
.aplay1 \flic\ipas\RAIN
.stop v

.vout conga3
.aplay1 \flic\fli\to10
.delay 300
.aplay1 \flic\fli\chess
.aplay1 \flic\fli\dragcave
.aplay1 \flic\fli\dragonb
.stop V

.vout mus8targ
.screen 1
.aplay1 \flic\fli\to18
.delay 300

.aplay1 \flic\fli\drop_it2
.aplay1 \flic\fli\bookspin
.sync V0
.aplay \flic\fli\venus
.stop v
.delay 25

.play dontkn
.vout helicopt
.aplay1 \flic\fli\bridgfly
.stop f
.stop v

.play rush
.aplay1 \flic\fli\chan5_1
.aplay1 \flic\fli\newtonlo
.stop f
.delay 25
.play crystal
.vout brook
```

(listing continues)

```
        .aplay1 \flic\fli\fish2
        .vout whatheck
        .aplay1 \flic\fli\fish3
        .stop v

        .vout newvoc
        .aplay1 \flic\fli\engines
        .stop v
        .aplay1 \flic\fli\kramer2
        .aplay1 \flic\fli\sprocket
        .stop f

        .screen 1
        .vout mus6targ
        .aplay1 \flic\fli\to08
        .delay 300
        .aplay1 \flic\fli\PROBE
        .aplay1 \flic\fli\SUN_EXp
        .aplay1 \flic\fli\MIS_STRK
        .aplay1 \flic\fli\EXP_SHIP
        .stop v

        .aplay1 \flic\fli\to02
        .delay 300
        .play corporat
        .aplay1 \flic\fli\icl
        .stop f

        .aplay1 \flic\fli\to01
        .vout mus5targ
        .delay 300
        .aplay1 \flic\fli\viv_pre
        .stop v
        .play rag_time
        .aplay1 \flic\fli\perpetua
        .stop f

        .aplay1 \flic\fli\to03
        .delay 300
        .play funky
        .aplay1 \flic\fli\CCDOBJC2
        .stop f
        .delay 25

        .play memories
        .aplay1 \flic\fli\DUST
        .aplay1 \flic\fli\CYCLE
        .aplay1 \flic\fli\TARGET
        .repeat 3
        .aplay1 \flic\fli\monfly
        .end
        .aplay1 \flic\fli\FRACTRO
        .aplay1 \flic\fli\fRACZOOM
        .stop f
```

```
.vout mus7targ
.aplay1 \flic\fli\to11
.delay 300
.aplay1 \flic\fli\robotrk
.stop v

.play highways
.aplay1 \flic\fli\to09
.delay 300
.aplay1 \flic\fli\CRATER
.delay 200
.stop f
.delay 25
.play drapes
.aplay1 \flic\fli\speafire

.aplay1 \flic\fli\to16
.delay 300
.aplay1 \flic\fli\CYCART_1
.aplay1 \flic\fli\PLAYROOM
.aplay1 \flic\fli\PLAYROOM
.aplay1 \flic\fli\scale
.aplay1 \flic\fl1\scale
.aplay1 \flic\fli\scale
.stop f

.vout mus4targ
.aplay1 \flic\fli\to19
.delay 300
.aplay1 \flic\fli\FLIGHT

.aplay1 \flic\fli\to20
.delay 300
.aplay1 \flic\fli\GUMBY
.aplay1 \flic\fli\BZOOM320
.vout mus1targ
.aplay1 \flic\fli\to15
.delay 300
.aplay1 \flic\fli\kickme
.stop v

.vout mus3targ
.aplay1 \flic\fli\to12
.delay 300
.aplay1 \flic\fli\LOWLOGO
.delay 50
.aplay1 \flic\fli\to13
.delay 300
.aplay1 \flic\fli\VIVIDSHP
.delay 50
.aplay1 \flic\fli\to05.fli
.delay 300
.aplay1 \flic\fli\FIGHTL.FLI
.stop v
```

(listing continues)

```
.play mozart1
.aplay1 \flic\fli\to22
.delay 300
.aplay1 \flic\fli\walk
.aplay1 \flic\fli\sprocket
.aplay1 \flic\fli\starglob

.play skywaltz
.aplay1 \flic\fli\tombrain
.aplay1 \flic\fli\aslamp
.aplay1 \flic\fli\carboard
.aplay1 \flic\fli\dude
.aplay1 \flic\fli\prop
.aplay1 \flic\fli\chopcity

.screen 1
.aplay1 \flic\fli\wfend
.stop f
```

Playing Large VOC Files with MMPLAY

Often the music played during MMPLAY scripts can be quite repetitive. This is because unlike flics, the digitized audio is loaded completely into memory all at once. One clever aspect of the Creative Labs VOC file format is that digitized sound can be broken up into any number of repeating blocks within the file. Thanks to this feature, a long piece of repetitive music can be stored in a small file that doesn't occupy much memory. This is how BIGDEMO is able to sustain the playing of the repetitive digitized music for so long while the flic files stream from disk.

If your MMPLAY script is to be played off a CD-ROM, timing animations and sounds can be a particularly laborious exercise. The problem is that flic files, the interesting ones at least, require a data transfer rate far in excess of the 150K per second maximum that most CD-ROM drives can achieve. Many CD-ROM drives on the market today still do not have an on-board hardware cache, so they can't achieve even this snail-like pace. Just because

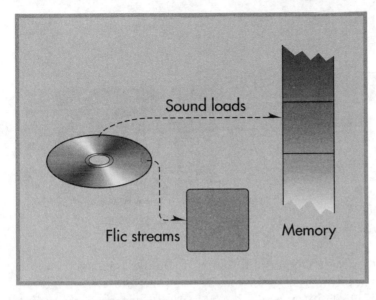

Figure 3-21 With MMPLAY digitized sound files are loaded into memory, but flic files are streamed from disk

your MMPLAY script may be synchronized perfectly playing from your hard disk, the chances are that your result will be entirely different when the sequence is played from CD-ROM as shown in Figure 3-21. The BIGDEMO flows as smoothly as it does because the flic files were already on a CD-ROM when the music was composed. Peter and Niko were able to synchronize the audio so accurately with the graphics only because they knew the playback speed of the FLIs from the disc.

While you were watching BIGDEMO, you may have noticed that the Sound Blaster can play sequenced music that isn't as repetitive as the digitized VOC files. The Yamaha FM chips on the Sound Blaster provide the capability of playing back sequences of notes that Creative Labs calls CMF or FM type music. On the original Sound Blaster and Sound Blaster Pro, this type of music had a depressingly tinny quality. The Sound Blaster Pro 2 now uses a more sophisticated Yamaha chip set, which gives it vastly enhanced sound quality.

FRACTAL ZOOM

by Starcom CDROM

Christian Menard

Size: 23MB

Memory: 500K free RAM

Keys: (CTRL)-(END) to quit

Figure 3-22 Starcom logo

We have one other MMPLAY script to share. If you like fractals, then this demo (as shown in Figure 3-22) is for you. By using WINFRACT, a Windows version of FRACTINT, and the Windows Macro Recorder, Christian has developed a beautiful technique for making a smooth fractal zoom. WINFRACT can be found in *The Waite Group's Fractals for Windows*, 1992.

To start this demo, choose **Starcom Fractal Zoom** from the **MMPLAY Scripts Menu**. This demo starts with a larger lengthy animation of the Starcom logo, which was created with Autodesk 3D Studio. For those of you who don't speak German, the word "Vertrieb" on the screen means "distribution." The ghosting illusion of the Starcom logo shrinking into the distance is created with the Trails effect in Autodesk Animator.

Note: To quit from the Fractal Zoom press (CTRL)-(END).

How to Make a Fractal Zoom Movie

WINFRACT is a very popular fractal-generation program developed by the Stone Soup Group. One of the nice features of this program is the ability to zoom into a fractal image by a fixed amount. To create a fractal zoom such as the one shown in Figure 3-23, just create a macro that zooms in and then saves the resultant image. If when recording your macro you move the boxed area before you render it, you will create a smoothly sliding zoom in the general direction you moved the box. Be careful not to push the zoom box toward the blue lake area or you will end up zooming into an area that doesn't contain anything worth seeing. Because the GIF format allows the

Figure 3-23 A Mandelbrot fractal

storing of information about the fractal formula in the picture itself, it is quite easy to change the direction in which the zoom moves by reloading any of the images and then re-recording the macro.

Fractal Movie Down and Dirty

We can easily create a fractal zoom (Figure 3-24), but first we must prepare a number of programs. Run WINFRACT and choose a fractal into which you wish to zoom. Save this image as a GIF with three zeros as the final three characters of the file name. Next, check the option Zoom Bar under

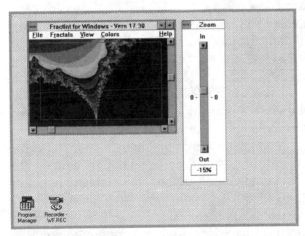

Figure 3-24 WINFRACT with Macro Recorder iconized and Zoom Bar open

the View menu so we can precisely adjust the amount by which we move into the fractal. From the Windows Program Manager, run the Macro Recorder and choose Record from the Macro menu. Choose a key to activate the macro and under Playback / Speed, choose Recorded Speed. With the Recorder minimized and flashing, change the Zoom amount by clicking on the arrow at the top of the Zoom window slider bar. Notice that as you alter the percentage by which to zoom, the box over the fractal resizes itself accordingly. After you have adjusted the size of the area, you can move the box so that it is centered on the area you want to explore. Double-clicking on this boxed image renders the fractal. Choose Save As from the File menu and choose OK to save. The file name is identical to the previous image you saved except that it is incremented by one digit. Next double-click on the Recorder icon to stop the recording procedure. If you choose to play back this macro continuously, you will create a series of GIF images that form a fractal zoom. This series of images can then be easily loaded into Autodesk Animator to create a flic file.

FAST, FASCINATING, AND FREQUENTLY FOREIGN SOUND BLASTER DEMOS

If the Swiss are the best at making clocks, the Japanese the best at making cars, and the Americans the best at making computers, then the Europeans are the best at making state-of-the-art, custom-coded, Sound Blaster demos.

In this section, we will explore some of the best PC demos from Europe, some screens of which are shown in Figure 3-25. The flashy bits are generally written in custom assembly language and accompanied by fairly advanced electronic MIDI and digitized music. The heavy-metal digital sound frequently borders on jarring, and the beat may be too heavy for long listening periods. But this approach makes a great self-running demo because it draws people in. As you will see, each of these teams tries to one up the next in the spirit of friendly competition. The result is that we have some graphics and sounds that will knock your socks off.

Readers familiar with the Commodore Amiga will immediately recognize the style of the demos described in this section. In its heyday a few years ago, legions of young hackers developed demos on this then-popular machine. Times have changed but unfortunately the Amiga hasn't. Although there have been myriad advances in PC technology, developments in the Amiga world have been relatively few. Today's young programmers tolerate DOS, Intel's segmented memory architecture, and the total absence

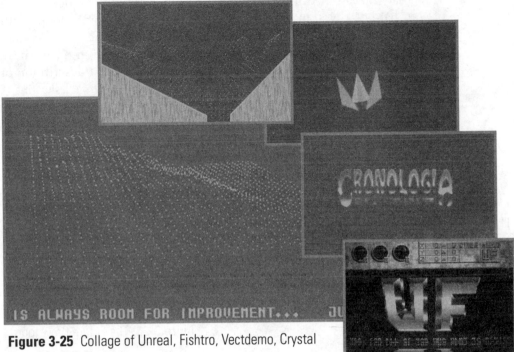

Figure 3-25 Collage of Unreal, Fishtro, Vectdemo, Crystal Dream, and Cronologia

of any hardware-assisted graphics routines because they can get so much more computing power for their money. Particularly in Europe, these youngsters seem to enjoy nothing more than figuring out new ways of pushing the limits of the PC. Ideas are shared via BBSs and at specially arranged gatherings known as demo parties. The Fishtro piece described below is an example of a demo that was created for the sole purpose of luring people to an event of this type called "Assembly 92." The demos in this section exhibit a level of excellence that is achieved only by people who truly love their work.

A Caveat

A little caveat is in order before we go any further. The demos in this section are right at the bleeding edge of multimedia. Their creators have broken every rule and used every trick necessary to squeeze the maximum performance from your PC. In general, these custom-coded demos want as much of DOS's 640K of memory as they can get. Consequently, you should try commenting out disk caching software and any other device drivers or

TSRs that you can. Because the best way to run some of these demos is off of your hard disk, you may want to boot your computer from a floppy with the minimum system on it. In order to facilitate this, the menu system provides an easy means of copying the most memory hungry of these demos to the hard disk and generating a boot floppy. For a description of this procedure, see **"Making a Boot Disk"** in Appendix B, *Troubleshooting*.

DEMOS FROM LAPLAND:
The Future Crew

Samuli Syvahuoko

Figure 3-26 The Future Crew logo

All nine members of the Future Crew, whose logo appears in Figure 3-26, are still in school as I write this book. Their ages range from 16 to 21. Their founder and assembly language programming guru Sami Tammilehto is currently studying computing at a university in his hometown of Turku, Finland. To understand how the Future Crew has risen to its undisputed position as the finest demo group in the world, a little history is in order.

History of the Future Crew

Sami started producing demos on a Commodore 64 in 1986. Soon after his purchase of a PC with a Sound Blaster in 1988, he released a music editing program called The Scream Tracker. This program was the first to be able to load, manipulate, and play back Amiga sound modules through the Sound Blaster. An enhanced version of the Scream Tracker was released in 1990 that utilized the Sound Blaster's DAC (digital analog converter) channel, radically improving the level of sound quality. Because this sounded so much better than music from the Adlib card, other developers focused on adding this feature to their software. To further assist other developers, in 1991 the Future Crew released a demo called *Mental Surgery* into the public domain *with full ASM source code.* The 3-D starfield, large scrolling text, and pulsing graphic equalizers were copied by many programmers around the world as they explored the inner workings of the Sound Blaster. You can find the latest version of the Scream Tracker in the file \SBDEMOS\FUTURE_C\SCREAM_T.ZIP on the CD. The Mental Surgery demo, along with full assembler source code, can be found in the same directory in the file MENTAL_S.ZIP.

Their latest demos are described in detail in the following sections. In the next year, they plan to start writing games for a U.S.-based company to break into the multimedia industry. Regardless, they intend to keep creating demos and distributing them for free because they have so much fun doing so. What they enjoy most of all is the competition and sharing of ideas with other groups in the demo community. The PC message networks of Europe used by these groups exude a spirit of cooperation that is quite difficult for the average secretive Silicon Valley software developer to understand. In fact, these kids laugh openly at the seriousness with which so many take computing. For them, it's all just a hobby. Perhaps their recognition of the risk of burn-out shows an aspect of wisdom beyond their years.

THE UNREAL DEMO

Size: 2.3MB of audio and graphics

Memory: 600K free RAM

CPU: 386 / 20 MHz or better

Keys: (CTRL)-(ESC) to quit, (ESC) to move ahead

This demo requires that your Sound Blaster be set at the default of IRQ 7.

Figure 3-27 The UNREAL logo

Have you ever run a program on your PC and said to yourself, "That's not possible! It can't be real"? Well, if this has never happened to you before, get ready. UNREAL, the opening screen of which can be seen in Figure 3-27, weighs in at a hefty 2.5MB, which is much larger than any of the other custom-coded Sound Blaster demos on the CD or known to mankind. Into that space, the Future Crew has managed to pack animated plasma clouds, pulsing oscilloscopes, full-motion flybys and numerous other breathtaking effects. And all these great graphics are set to some thrilling music. This spectacular demo is quite demanding with regard to machine resources. Many of the effects only work smoothly on a fast 386 or above PC. Also, if you don't have 600K of free DOS memory, you will have to follow the procedure for making a boot disk described in Appendix B, *Troubleshooting*, to get this masterpiece rolling.

Starting UNREAL

Assuming that you do have 600K of free DOS memory with your CD-ROM drivers loaded and at least 2.5MB of free hard disk space, select **Unreal** from **Future Crew Productions Submenu,** which you will find as an option under **Demos for the Sound Blaster.** Because this demo loads so much faster from a hard disk, you will be asked for a drive letter onto which to copy the file. The drive letter you choose will be checked for available disk space and if sufficient space is found, the demo will be copied. If the chosen drive doesn't have enough disk space, you will be informed of this before being returned to the menu. Once copied, UNREAL.EXE executes immediately. Upon being presented with the opening menu, as shown in Figure 3-28, select a playback frequency by moving the highlighted bar with the arrow keys. Choosing a higher

This presentation requires a **386** computer. A **486** is strongly recommended! The demo runs perfectly on **486/33Mhz** with **Tseng Labs SuperVGA**, and still smoothly on a fast 386. Below that, some parts run at a slower speed. For better results, try lowering sound quality or completely disabling sound. Please try removing all un-necessary residents (**especially disk caches**) if you encounter problems.

No sound	SoundBlaster	SoundBlaster Pro	SoundMaster II
44.1Khz	8Khz	**8Khz stereo**	8Khz
96.2Mhz	16Khz	16Khz stereo	16Khz
100.1Mhz	20Khz	20Khz stereo	20Khz

Press **ENTER** to start the presentation

Press **ESC** to quit now or skip parts later

Press **CTRL-ESC** later to quit to dos

Figure 3-28 The UNREAL opening menu

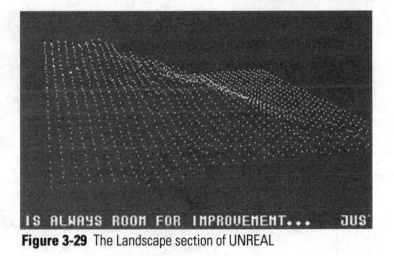

Figure 3-29 The Landscape section of UNREAL

playback frequency will improve the sound quality but will slow down the graphics. We suggest that you choose the default of 8KHz so that as much of the PC's resources can be devoted to the graphics as possible. Choosing a higher playback frequency doesn't improve the already superb sound quality all that much. Press (ENTER) to get the show on the road.

UNREAL opens with a spinning Finnish flag tumbling through an accurate starfield. Just as the rising music reaches it crescendo, the Future Crew logo appears. At each successive crescendo of the music, the credits appear in spectacular fashion, until the UNREAL logo bursts into the center of the screen as the starfield collapses. The music then changes and we are led into the first of the eight sections of this incredible demo.

You can press (ESC) at any time if you want to skip ahead. (CTRL)-(ESC) will terminate the demo and return you to the menu system or DOS.

Don't bail out until you see the finale, called Landscape, as shown in Figure 3-29. You'll be taken on a flight over 3-D terrain that is like nothing you have ever seen on a microcomputer of any type before. When asked which part of UNREAL the Future Crew was the most proud of, the response was the unique routines used to create this incredible effect developed by Mika Tuomi.

Figure 3-30 Opening screen of THEPARTY

How Future Crew Makes Demos

Creating a demo like UNREAL is a long complicated process only possible with a well-organized division of labor. Some members of the group focus on programming while others produce graphics or compose music. The length of time required to produce a demo like UNREAL is dependent upon two main things. The first of these is whether or not original effects are desired. Recycling existing assembler code is much quicker than writing new routines from scratch. The other factor is the length of the demo. Considering how long UNREAL runs, it should come as no surprise that it took over a year to produce. An example of a demo that took only two weeks would be THEPARTY, as seen in Figure 3-30, which you will find as an option in the **Future Crew Productions Menu.**

Once a new idea for an effect is conceived, it is first prototyped in C or Pascal. The prototype is then judged as either being worthy of optimization in assembly language or is discarded. The key thing that the Future Crew decides is whether or not the optimized routine will be fast enough to create an outstanding effect. Speed is everything to this group. The members admit that really fast assembler effects have been judged to be very popular even when the graphics and sound aren't quite up to snuff. This optimization stage usually takes three times as long as the creation of the C or Pascal prototype.

FISHTRO – WHAT A UNIQUE INVITATION TO A PARTY!

.531MB of audio and graphics

Memory: 500K free RAM

CPU: 386 / 20 MHz or better

Keys: (CTRL)-(ESC) to quit

(ESC) to advance to the next section

Figure 3-31 Screen from FISHTRO

The second demo by the Future Crew included on *Walkthroughs & Flybys CD* was created to publicize a gathering held in Finland of the young creative minds that make these incredible demos. You can run this demo by selecting **FISHTRO** from the **Future Crew Productions Menu**. As with UNREAL, a batch file will copy this demo to your hard disk and execute it from there because loading from the CD is so slow.

The best way to describe this piece is as a cute and busy digital aquarium, as can be seen in Figure 3-31. Even adults will squeal with delight at the animated figures of fish, eels, and lemmings. And there are so many of these figures and other effects that your eyes won't know where to look. All of this is set to a catchy watery song that reinforces the imagery very well. Here's a blow-by-blow description of what you'll see.

Particle System Effects

The demo fades up from black revealing a pipe surrounded by cascading water. Messages fly into the middle of the screen. The characters are composed of dozens of small dots flying in formation, as seen in Figure 3 32. These dots bounce off the walls of the pipe and fall to the bottom of the screen as if drawn to it by gravity. Because this effect is repeated to display three different messages, we get a nice look at the accurate trajectory of each of the particles. After the third message is displayed, the screen fades to black and the main feature begins.

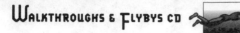

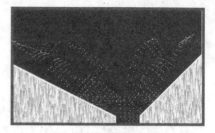

Figure 3-32 FISHTRO opening
with particle effects

You'll find yourself looking at a rapidly filling pond complete with rocks covered in green slime. The strangest thing about this pond has to be the big stereo sitting on the bottom. As the waves rise, more and more of the background is translucently dulled. Just as the watery music starts, fish swim out from behind the rocks and lights begin to dance on the display panels of the stereo.

Sensory Overload

There is motion on the cones of the speakers, the equalizer on the stereo is pulsing, water is continuing to drip out of the pipe while messages are being displayed in two different parts of the screen with two totally different styles. The most interesting figures to watch are the beautifully drawn fish of different sizes and colors. One fish is a spoof of Robocop shrouded in armor plating while another is wearing sunglasses. Lemmings join the fish after the first 30 seconds, and they all swim together as one big happy family. Too bad the larger fish don't devour the smaller fish, but I guess that wasn't part of the spec. The more closely you look at this demo, the more there is to see.

Be sure to notice how beautifully the text is handled in FISHTRO. The messages in the middle of the screen look as if each pixel of every letter is being blown into place and then away by a strong breeze. The manner in which the dots chaotically swirl and re-form implores you to read the text much more than a static display would do. You will also notice that another set of messages is being written across the sky at the top of the screen. This text appears in a multicolored font before it bursts into white and fades into the graduated background with a subtle shift of the palette.

VECTDEMO

from Ultraforce

Ultra Force Software Development

Eric Oostendorp

.293MB of audio and graphics

CPU: 386 or better

Keys: (ESC) to quit

Figure 3-33 Ultraforce logo over trees

The Ultraforce team is comprised of six self-described computer maniacs who thrive on writing games, utilities, and demos that push the PC to its limits. Their most impressive demo so far is VECTDEMO which opens to the Ultraforce logo rising from behind some trees, as seen in Figure 3-33. A pulsing beat starts as the large, shiny metallic letters UF spin up from the bottom of the screen. The speed at which the objects in this demo rotate with pseudo-reflection is nothing short of phenomenal. On a fast 386, the currently rotating object will be reflected in water along the bottom of the screen.

Some of the rotating objects are rather complex and traverse across up to 3/4 of your monitor. These shapes vary from a burial casket to an MTV logo to just a simple cube. There are figures of a man, woman, and dog formed out of nothing but shaded spheres. It is interesting to note that all of the spheres have the same reflective spot and that only a few sizes exist. The rotating objects are warped by such an extreme perspective that they appear to curve away in a most unnatural manner.

Interactivity

What sets VECTDEMO apart from the other custom programmed Sound Blaster demos is its interactivity. Pressing the (SPACEBAR) causes a control panel, which can be seen in Figure 3-34, to drop down from the top of the screen. Three dials on the panel indicate the rotation speeds of the three separate axes. Table 3-1 lists the keys you can use to alter the rotation.

Figure 3-34 VECTDEMO control panel

TABLE 3-1 VECTDEMO ROTATION KEYS

Key	Function
(SPACEBAR)	Toggles control panel display.
(F1) – (F2)	Changes the rotation speed of the X-axis.
(F3) – (F4)	Changes the rotation speed of the Y-axis.
(F5) – (F6)	Changes the rotation speed of the Z-axis.
(F7) – (F8)	Changes the distance from the object.
(F9) – (F10)	Loads a new rotating object.

CRYSTAL DREAM

by Triton

Triton

Magnus Hogdahl

1.4MB of graphics and audio

Memory: 500K free RAM

CPU: 286 or better

Keys: There is no way to quit this demo

This demo doesn't run on the Sound Blaster 16.

Figure 3-35 Crystal Dream

This Swedish-based group has produced an outstanding 16-color Sound Blaster demo. After selecting **Crystal Dream by Triton** from **The Sound**

Blaster Demos Menu, you'll be presented with the opening screen. Choose the menu option for your Sound Blaster depending upon whether it is the standard or Pro version. Use the 30KHz replay rate as the other options seem to have little effect.

The opening of Crystal Dream is like a journey through space, as seen in Figure 3-35. What's unique about this starfield is the way the camera swings around the various sides of the spaceship, the entire universe rotating with it. A blue square comes flying at us that fills the screen with a strange flowing plasma design for a few seconds before it peels away as a facet of a morphing geometric shape. This shape gently changes color as it alters its geometry while continuing to tumble through space. Numerous other objects fly past our view with uncanny smoothness. There is even an unusual space station that completely fills the display as it pans across the screen.

Checkerboard bases are widespread in the world of 3-D demos. Although they can get boring after a while, in Crystal Dream we have a new twist. The shadows of translucent shapes display the correct hues on the checkerboard, which is pretty amazing considering that the demo is running in only 16 colors (Figure 3-36). The finale is a number of still and animated raytraced images that are nice, but they don't approach the quality produced by programs like Big-D and POV-Ray.

The major failing of Crystal Dream is that there is no way out of this demo short of pressing the reset button or watching it through to the end. As was mentioned in the introduction to this section, these demo developers use any trick they can to get more performance from the PC. To increase the speed of Crystal Dream, Triton doesn't poll the keyboard until

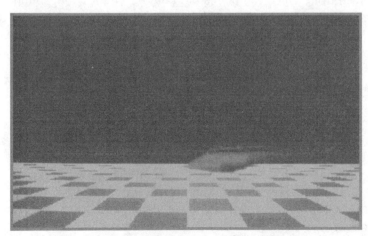

Figure 3-36 Checkerboard landscape of Crystal Dream

the credits appear. Once the demo reaches that point, you can press the (ESC) key to quit. If you do power your machine off to quit, make sure that your hard disk is not being accessed as you throw the switch or you could potentially damage your computer.

An unusual trick ending occurs with Crystal Dream. Upon exiting, you'll see a DOS prompt displayed on the screen showing your current directory. However, you're not yet at DOS, and as soon as you press any key a message flies across the screen in text mode that says, "We'll be back." This is not a virus, but just a little ploy to get your attention.

CRONOLOGIA

by Cascada

Cascada

Erik Stridell

.474MB of audio and graphics

Memory: 500K free RAM

CPU: 286 or better

Keys: (ESC) to proceed to the next section

Figure 3-37 Cronologia opening screen

Cronologia, a screen from which can be seen in Figure 3-37, is a long demo that has some clever parts and great music. Start this demo by choosing **Cronologia by Cascada** from **The Sound Blaster Demos Menu**. If you choose "Use the last sound card setup?" for this demo, it will run configured for a Sound Blaster Pro in the factory default settings of I/O address 220 and IRQ 7. If you have another sound card, just answer the questions describing your system settings.

Don't be alarmed that there is no sound for the first 20 seconds or so while the credits appear. The demo proper starts with colored horizontal bars beating to the music, while the Cascada logo smoothly glides from side to side. On occasion, the beating colored bars change into an undulating mode where they fly up and down the screen in formation. Note the messages that are scrolling across the bottom of the screen and how the tail of the large Cascada logo is cut off when it intrudes into this scrolling area. After a while, the center of the Cascada logo spreads down to black and the members of the team appear one after another. When the programmer's picture appears, the undulating bars go into high speed mode as if he's showing off the best he can do.

Between the sections of Cronologia, red text slithers across the screen announcing that a new set of effects are loading into memory. Any time during this demo, you can press the (ESC) key to proceed to the next section. The second part of Cronologia is called vectors and it features the smooth movement of various 3-D objects accompanied by a running commentary along the bottom of the screen. After five minutes or so of this we get our first gag. Poking fun at its rival groups (whose demos we have described), Cascada flies the flags of Holland and Finland across the screen after asking the question, "Who makes the best demo?" Of course, this is followed by the Swedish flag.

The third section of this demo is the most harsh. The music has a hard, grating beat that is matched by bright, full-screen jarring graphics. In this section, five different types of effects are repeated over and over again in time with the music. While the level of control that they show is impressive, the end result is disturbing enough that you wouldn't want to watch this demo just before going to sleep for fear of bad dreams. This section finishes with the music and images speeding up to the point at which they begin to overload the system. There is a brilliant explosion and the screen changes to static just like on TV.

The credits in this demo, as seen in Figure 3-38, are just great. Balls gently flowing through various geometrically shaped paths form the background for the final messages. The soothing music and hypnotic screen effects so starkly contrast the previous section that this demo has what can only be described as a great ending.

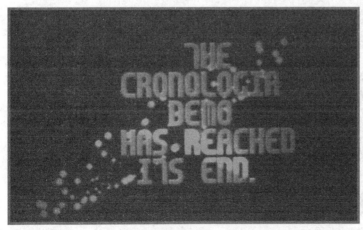

Figure 3-38 Cronologia credits

WING COMMANDER II

by Origin Systems

Origin Systems

3.5MB of audio and graphics
Memory: 580K free RAM and EMS needed
CPU: 386 or better
No keys are active. Reset to exit

Figure 3-39 Wing Commander II demo

This demo for one of the most popular flight simulation games around demonstrates that Origin Systems (whose logo appears in the demo opener, Figure 3-39) has graphics synchronized with sound down to a fine art. To run this demo, choose **Wing Commander II demo by Origin** from **The Sound Blaster Demos Menu.** You'll need EMS memory, so if it doesn't run correctly from the menu system, follow the procedure to boot from a floppy disk described in Appendix B, *Troubleshooting.*

Notice that this demo uses only the middle 75% of the screen, which creates a subtle cinematic effect that draws the viewer in. After the orchestra

Figure 3-40 The talking cat-like figure

finishes tuning up, there are some fireworks announcing the start of the demo. Great Star Wars-like music plays as a small space ship appears navigating its way through an asteroid belt. The music creates an aura of anticipation and adventure as we find ourselves hurtling toward the headquarters ship. You can tell from the smooth manner in which all of the elements of the screen move in harmony that the creators of this demo are seasoned pros. Once aboard the headquarters ship, we are ushered into a meeting with the leader of this cat-like race of space warriors, one of which is shown in Figure 3-40. As we hear the figures speak, their mouths move just enough to create a lip-synched effect.

I love the Wing Commander II demo because there is a story being told. None of the other Sound Blaster demos we have shown you have a theme and this is a real shame. For me, the ideal Sound Blaster demo would have a great story line, like Wing Commander II, combined with the effects of UNREAL, and the interactivity of VECTDEMO. Wouldn't that be a winning combination!

CHAPTER 4

THE AUTODESK WORLD
OF 3-D MOVIES

In this chapter, we will look at movies created with 3D Studio from Autodesk Multimedia Division. This single product, the packaging for which can be seen in Figure 4-1, has changed the landscape of the demo industry forever by providing an easy means for creating full-motion animations of photorealistic quality. With Autodesk 3D Studio and a 386-class PC, anyone with an artistic flair can create his own walkthroughs and flybys. This chapter will first explain a bit about the concept of differential

Figure 4-1 Photo of Autodesk 3D Studio

animation and the evolution of the flic file format before taking a look at the main concepts of 3D Studio. You'll be introduced to the power of IPAS external procedures and their dazzling ability to create life. The remainder of the chapter is devoted to in-depth discussions of particular flics created with Autodesk and non-Autodesk software.

THE PRINCIPLE OF DIFFERENTIAL ANIMATION

Images that must be displayed in rapid succession on a PC are usually sent to the screen as a rectangular area of pixels, or bits. If you look at a typical computer movie, you'll notice that areas of the screen remain unchanged between each frame. This fact can be exploited so that just the differences between subsequent frames are stored. The technique of playing back only these differences is known as *delta* or *differential* animation. The illustration shown in Figure 4-2 will help you to visualize how this works. The Δ character symbolizes just the changes from frame to frame.

Even though the GRASP authoring language supported differential animations for a couple of years before Autodesk Animator, it wasn't until Animator came along that the differential technique became

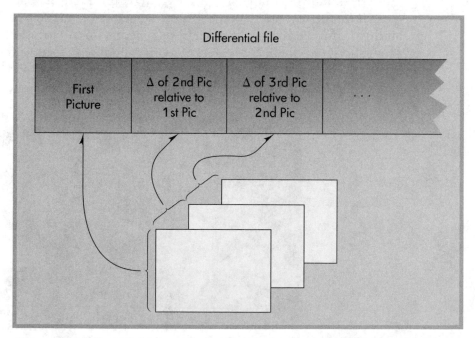

Figure 4-2 Differential animation records the changes between frames

widespread on the PC. Although GRASP could consolidate a series of pictures into a differential, it provided no easy way to create the individual frames. Animator changed that by being specifically designed to create and edit pictures in a series as an animation. With Animator, the many functions of a paint program can just as easily apply to a range of pictures as they can to any single one. Coupling this new concept with all of the other features of Animator raised the level of what is possible with PC demos to a new height.

Flic Files — The Standard Format for Bitmapped Animation

The FLI file format as introduced with Autodesk Animator was restricted to a VGA mode of displaying 256 colors at a 320x200 screen resolution. There were two main advantages with this low resolution for Animator version 1.0, the most important of these being performance related. The Intel-based 80x86 processors (8088, 286, 386, and 486) are all designed to move data in 64K chunks. Because the memory required to hold an image of the screen at VGA resolution is less than that of a single 64K data segment, fast moving, full-screen graphics can be achieved much more efficiently at this low resolution mode than at the higher resolutions. The vertical bar in

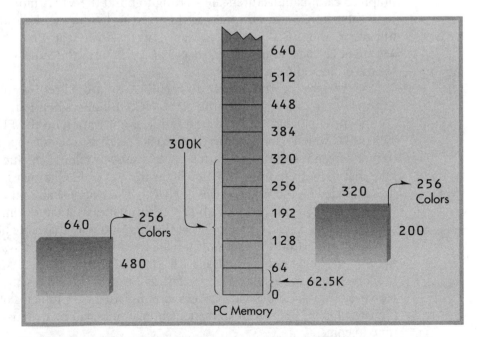

Figure 4-3 A screen at 320x200 resolution is less than a 64K data segment

Figure 4-3 represents the computer's memory. As you can see, a single screen at the 320x200x256 color resolution fits into a 64K data segment. At 640x480x256 colors, a single screen requires 300K of memory, an amount that requires five different data segments to be accessed.

The second reason was that any color VGA equipped PC could run Animator, which gave the product a wide base. If Animator had been restricted only to 640x480x256 SuperVGA systems, Autodesk would have had trouble supporting all of the different graphics cards as they became available. It is important to realize that when Animator was being developed the market for SuperVGA graphics adapters was a real mess of conflicting standards and incompatibility.

VESA Saves the Day

Thanks to the Video and Electronics Standards Association (VESA), the compatibility issue is now much more straightforward. This group established a standard interface through which programmers can detect and set SuperVGA modes, providing that the PC is VESA compliant. At this time it is usually necessary to load a small resident utility in order to make a PC compatible with the VESA standard. The good news is that more and more graphics card manufacturers are starting to build the VESA modes directly into their hardware, eliminating the need to load a resident utility. By adopting the VESA standard early, with Animator Pro, Autodesk Multimedia Division helped blaze a clear path out of the SuperVGA jungle for the entire industry.

The release of the more powerful Animator Pro extended the functionality of the program to SuperVGA modes when run on VESA compliant PCs. This release also introduced a variation on the FLI format called FLC which offers improved playback speed, as well as support for the higher screen resolutions. (In this book when we refer to *flic* files, please take that to mean movies stored in either the FLI or FLC format.) The FLC files included on the *Walkthroughs & Flybys CD* are almost all in the popular 640x480 screen resolution. Full-screen animations of larger dimensions require so much screen memory that they tend to play unevenly on all but the most powerful PCs. Certainly advances in local bus video systems are helping to alleviate these bottlenecks. Some of the new 486/50MHz local bus machines can display FLCs as fast as FLIs on the slower processors. However, until local bus video grows in popularity, the problems of playing high-resolution, full-screen animations in real time will be with us for some time to come.

3D STUDIO BRINGS BROADCAST QUALITY TO THE DESKTOP

The developers of Autodesk 3D Studio, The Yost Group, have a long history in developing software for different microcomputers. Their expertise has translated not just into an incredibly powerful 3-D visualization and animation system, as can be seen in Figure 4-4, but also one that is well thought out and quite straightforward. While explaining the features and operations of this program in any depth at all is well beyond the purpose of this book, it is important to describe the program in at least a cursory fashion to give you some idea of how the animations you will see are created. By understanding the basic approach that this program takes, you'll be better equipped to understand and evaluate other programs that perform a similar function.

Autodesk 3D Studio is comprised of five integrated modules:

- The 2D Shaper provides tools for creating and editing 2-D designs, including those imported from other systems via the AutoCAD DXF file format. Powerful Bezier fonts give complete control over the creation of 3-D text. Polygons can be distorted in a variety of ways such as bending, tapering, and scaling.

Figure 4-4 The 3D Studio city scene from the Release 2.0 packaging

- The 3D Lofter converts 2-D shapes into 3-D models through the use of spline-based extrusion paths. By spline-based, we mean that the path the 2-D shape follows as it becomes a 3-D object doesn't have to be linear. For example, a corkscrew shaped object could be created by lofting a circle along a path the shape of a helix. One of the most powerful features of the lofter is the Fit command that creates 3-D objects from horizontal and vertical cross sections.

- The 3D Editor provides the environment for editing, assembling, and manipulating the scene. Cameras and lights are used to create shadows and perspective. Rendering then provides a photorealistic image which may be overlaid against a scanned picture or graduated background.

- The Materials Editor allows you to create or modify surface qualities of your objects by adjusting the color and shininess or by applying texture, bump, opacity, and reflection maps. Using these capabilities, it is possible to create a variety of realistic surface finishes such as glass, wood, stone, metal, and plastic.

- The Keyframer enables you to animate your model with full interactive control over movement, lighting, and camera angles. Objects within an animation can be morphed to transform from one shape to another. Hierarchical linking allows a child object to inherit the motions of a parent, radically simplifying the creation of complex sequences. The finished result can be used to create an animation file for replaying on the PC or it can be recorded directly to video.

Viewing FLI Files on the CD with AAPLAY

We are going to deviate a bit from our description of 3D Studio in order to get you running flics as soon as possible. The viewer you are about to run, AAPLAY.EXE, is the freely distributable player that Autodesk includes with Animator version 1.0. Here is a list of the menu selections that you need to choose in order to run AAPLAY directly from the CD. From the Main Menu choose:

Autodesk 3D Studio Animations, then choose
320x200 FLIs, then choose
Load AAPLAY to view a particular FLI file

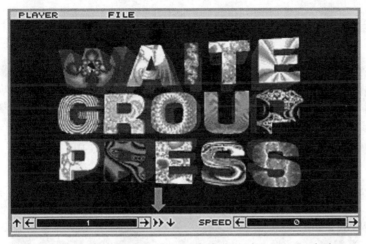

Figure 4-5 AAPLAY with a file loaded; note the arrow pointing to the play symbol

Once AAPLAY is running, move the mouse cursor so that it is located over the word **FILE** in the bar at the top of the screen. From the drop-down menu, choose **FLI LOAD**. At the bottom of the screen, a list of files will appear in a scroll box. Load a file from the list by double-clicking over the name with your mouse. To play the loaded file, click your mouse over the two triangles that symbolize play. The large arrow in Figure 4-5 will help you to locate the play symbol in AAPLAY.

Into the Future with IPAS

When asked what was missing from 3D Studio Release 2.0, one of the animators whose work we will see said, "I pass!" He meant that thanks to the power of the IPAS interface for external processes, anything that might have been left out can be added. IPAS programs are "plug-in" modules that extend the functionality of 3D Studio, allowing it to create such wonders as fractal forests, realistic explosions, and falling snow. There are four types of IPAS routines (I, P, A, and S):

- IXPs are **I**mage processing external procedures that manipulate images after they have been fully rendered. Sample IXPs are available to simulate the glowing of a jet engine exhaust or the flare of a lens when it is pointed directly toward the sun.

- PXPs are **P**rocedural modeling external processes that create or manipulate mesh geometry. Sample PXPs can be used to spherify, melt, wave, or twist existing objects. The IPAS programs for creating fractal planets and foliage fall into this category.

- AXPs are **A**nimated stand-in external processes, all aspects of which are created procedurally as the scene is being rendered. Sample AXPs create rain that splatters upon impact, fireworks that burst into the shapes of letters, and star fields that move at warp speed. AXP processes give 3D Studio the capability to generate full particle systems, a feature which up till now has only existed on the most expensive hardware platforms.

- SXPs are **S**olid texture external processes that give true depth to materials. This type of process is used to create a planet surface, realistic swirling smoke, or water.

Like AutoCAD, 3D Studio is an open system for which the development of add-ons is encouraged. Since Autodesk prefers developers to market their own add-on products, The Yost Group and Schreiber Instruments have teamed up to bring the first set of these, the IPAS Boutique, to market. Their five-package set costs $300 per package. (See Appendix C, *Sources*, for ordering details.)

Viewing the IPAS Flics on the *Walkthroughs & Flybys CD*

On the CD, the IPAS animations have been broken into two categories based on the two variations of the flic file format. We'll start by looking at the 320x200 FLI format files, as they stream from the CD much better than the higher resolution FLCs do. From the *Walkthroughs & Flybys CD* Main Menu choose:

Autodesk 3D Studio Animations Menu, then choose
320x200 FLIs created with IPAS

You will then be given three options for viewing the FLI files:

1. Play a script viewing each of the IPAS animations in turn. This script will loop, allowing the animations to play indefinitely until the (ESC) key is pressed,

2. Loop each IPAS animation until a key is pressed. Pressing (ESC) will return you to the menu system, or

3. Load the AAPLAY flic player so that you can individually choose which IPAS FLI files you want to view yourself.

IPAS Animations in the FLI Format

Often the size of a FLI file can give a good indication of how spectacular a particular animation will be. Because the AAPLAY utility provides no way for you to know the size of FLI files, this information has been included in Table 4-1.

TABLE 4-1 320X200 IPAS FLIC FILES LOCATED IN THE \FLIC\IPAS DIRECTORY

File Name	Size (Bytes)
BLUR.FLI	114290
CLAMP.FLI	271141
CRUMPLE.FLI	216974
DISINT.FLI	491662
EXPLODE.FLI	507854
EXPLODE2.FLI	688357
EXPLOD_5.FLI	692356
FIREWKS.FLI	489466
FLARE.FLI	387340
GLOW.FLI	271184
HILITE.FLI	219667
IPASFWRK.FLI	1154050
MELT.FLI	228186
MWAVE.FLI	149197
MWAVE_1.FLI	151394
PLANET.FLI	212021
PLASMA.FLI	104576
RAIN.FLI	396856
RAIN_2.FLI	243932
RESHAPE.FLI	191190
SKLINE.FLI	179493
SMOKE.FLI	267744
SNOW.FLI	391506
SPHIFY.FLI	313835
SPIRAL01.FLI	300404
SPIRAL02.FLI	317218
SPURT.FLI	273921
STRETCH.FLI	227688
TWIST.FLI	227424
WATER.FLI	469734
XMAS.FLI	10572

Short Descriptions of a Few IPAS FLI Files

Here are brief descriptions of some of the IPAS FLI files. These represent only a few of the more interesting flics, as it's impossible to pick out the best ones because they are all so good!

Figure 4-6

FLARE.FLI (See Figure 4-6.) This file shows how effectively the optical physics of a multi-element zoom lens can be simulated. This effect has 25 different options for controlling such things as the number of lens elements, the flare color, flare density, as well as automatic brightening of the scene during flare peaks.

Figure 4-7

DISINT.FLI (See Figure 4-7.) A bottle disintegrates into hundreds of particles that fall to the ground. The user can control such factors as the number of particles, the strength of gravity, and the springiness of the object.

Figure 4-8

MWAVE.FLI (See Figure 4-8.) This flic of an eerie, undulating ripple is created with the Mwave procedural add-on. A simple sine wave-shaped wire frame template encompasses the object you want to morph. Through a dialog box, you can control all the characteristics of the wave to give an undulating motion that is incredibly real.

Figure 4-9

RAIN.FLI (See Figure 4-9.) A number of water particles fall to the ground and splatter realistically on impact. The user can control parameters such as the number of rain particles, their size relative to the distance they have to drop, the number of frames before the pattern repeats, as well as various wind characteristics.

To give you a feel for the kind of controls that IPAS provides, more than 50 screen shots of the dialog boxes can be found in the \FLIC\IPAS directory. These screens are all stored in the GIF file format and can be viewed with any standard GIF decoding program.

Playing SuperVGA IPAS Animations

In this section, we will see the capabilities of IPAS at the higher 640x480x256 resolution. Viewing these FLC files, which are in the Animator Pro specific format, from the *Walkthroughs & Flybys CD* requires a bit more patience than viewing FLI files. The Trilobyte PLAY viewer used to play these animations must first load them entirely into memory before they are displayed on the screen. While this can take a moment or two, the effect of having the flic play at full speed from RAM is much more spectacular than when the data transfer rate is constrained by streaming from a CD-ROM or hard disk.

To speed up the loading process, we have provided a menu option to copy all of the flics, a total of 25.7MB, to your hard disk. After the files are copied, the Trilobyte PLAY viewer will then load and play them each in turn in a fraction of the time that it would take the PLAY viewer to load them from the CD.

 **Tip:** Because these animations require the 640x480x256 mode, you must have a VESA compliant SuperVGA in order for the Trilobyte PLAY viewer to function properly. See Appendix B, *Troubleshooting*, for information regarding VESA drivers. If your system has less than 8MB of RAM, some of these animations will stream from the CD or hard disk because they will be unable to load into the available memory.

To see these flics, make the following selections from the *Walkthroughs & Flybys CD* Main Menu:

Autodesk 3D Studio Animations Menu, then
640x480 FLCs, then choose either
Copy 25.7MB to Hard Disk or **Play FLC files from the CD**

If you have chosen to copy the FLCs to the hard disk, you will have to wait at least 3 minutes before any animations begin to play. (This delay assumes that you have a CD-ROM drive capable of streaming 150K per second. 300K per second drives will naturally take half this amount of time.) In Table 4-2, which follows, is a list of the five IPAS flic files and their sizes in the order that they will be played.

TABLE 4-2 SUPERVGA IPAS FLIC FILES LOCATED IN THE \FLIC\FLC DIRECTORY

File Name	Size (Bytes)
MANTA.FLC	1580430
DISINT.FLC	7776580
EXPLCYL.FLC	5493494
FWORKS1.FLC	6574512
WARP_ICE.FLC	4655588

Here are some of the more amazing IPAS FLC files that you will see in this script.

Figure 4-10

DISINT.FLC (See Figure 4-10.) This shows the effect of the Disintegration IPAS routine upon a representation of the Venus de Milo. A myriad number of balls in the shape of the statue wobble in place briefly before falling to the ground under the effect of an artificial gravity. Notice how realistically the tree grows in the background.

Figure 4-11

MANTA.FLC (See Figure 4-11.) A mechanical submarine swims with the grace of a fish thanks to the power of the MWAVE IPAS routine. If you are interested in animations that mimic life, don't miss this flic.

Figure 4-12

WARP_ICE.FLC (See Figure 4-12.) The effect of moving at warp speed through a universe of ice was created with the RAIN.AXP particle system generator. The size of the rain particles was set to be very large and the camera was placed on the ground pointed upwards.

ANIMATIONS CREATED WITH 3D STUDIO

Now that you have seen the latest capabilities of 3D Studio, get ready to examine a few spectacular animations up close and personal. In the next few pages, we will introduce a number of the world's leading 3-D animators and showcase their finest work. You'll learn how these experts approach the process of visualizing what they can only imagine. The subject matter in this section ranges from running human figures to exploding stars. On the serious side, you'll marvel at a 29MB fly-through of an office interior being built before your eyes. The animations you have seen up till now have been created for the most part by the program's designers at Autodesk. Now it's time to meet the enthusiasts who use 3D Studio to pay the rent.

Playing Flic Files in Standard VGA Format (FLI)

All of the files in this section are in the Animator 1.0 FLI format. To view them, run AAPLAY.EXE from the *Walkthroughs & Flybys CD* Main Menu. To do this, first choose:

> **Autodesk 3D Studio Animations Menu,** then choose
> **320x200 FLI Files,** then choose
> **Load AAPLAY** to view a particular FLI file

For instructions on using AAPLAY.EXE to load FLI files, see the earlier section "Viewing FLI files on the CD with AAPLAY."

A Perpetual Motion Machine

Adam Maitland
Virtual Image Ltd.

PERPETUA.FLI   14.8MB

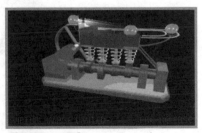

Figure 4-13 Screen shot of PERPETUA.FLI

Adam's first contract involving CAD was to create a wiring chart for a large arena sound system installation. At that point, he had no experience whatsoever with AutoCAD but thought he'd give it a go. Such a brash move typifies his outrageous character. After many years of playing the saxophone with bands in the United Kingdom and France, Adam got his start in computers experimenting with digital music. His approach to 3-D graphics has always been from an artist's perspective and it certainly shows.

Created entirely in 3D Studio Release 1.0, PERPETUA.FLI (Figure 4-13) is one of the largest flics on the CD, comprised of 1,981 frames and weighing in at a hefty 14.8MB. The repeating loop of the animating model (i.e., one ball making a complete circuit of the machine) is 360 frames long. Even though this animation was created in late 1990, Adam still considers it to be one of his most challenging projects.

The first thing to understand as you watch PERPETUA is that 3D Studio has no features to detect collisions between objects. The program provides no way for you to tell if two objects are occupying the same space short of rendering up the image and having a look.

The first parts of the model to be built were the camshaft and rods. By taking a view of the shaft end on, the vertical positions of a single rod were set to coincide with the height of the cam as it rotated. Since 3/4 of the circumference of the cam is round, the vertical positions for the rod only needed to be set for 1/4 of the frames of the sequence. Once a single rod was moving perfectly in sync with the cam, the rod was then cloned three times and the clones moved to their new positions. These new arms were then assigned the same set of vertical keys as the master arm with the Copy Tracks command.

The other tricky parts of PERPETUA were creating the rails and getting the balls to realistically roll along on top. Figure 4-14 is a close-up of this

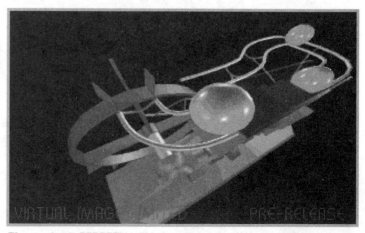

Figure 4-14 PERPETUA.FLI showing the rails

part of the animation. The important thing to realize here is that the same lofting path (the line in space along which something is extruded) that was used to create the rails was also used to assign the initial positions of the balls. While using the same lofting path assured that the balls would follow the track, the speed had to be manually adjusted. For example, notice how the ball bounces around a bit as it comes off the top piston. As with the rods, once the motion of the ball was correct, it was cloned twice to create the other two balls.

Be sure to view the VIV_PRE.FLI file which was also created by Adam Maitland.

An Office Growing Out of Plans Mapped to the Floor

Jamie Clay
Autodesk Multimedia Division

KRAMER2.FLI   6MB
KRAMER.FLI   29MB

Figure 4-15 KRAMER.FLI

This functional piece of animation starts with a camera panning through an empty, modern office. Through the large windows the brown rolling hills of Marin County, California, home to Autodesk's Multimedia Division, are clearly visible. The carpet then fades out to reveal a blueprint on the floor showing the arrangement of an office. Suddenly, partitions begin to rise out of the floor plan followed by furniture and plants. No other flic file on the *Walkthroughs & Flybys CD* better shows off the power of 3D Studio to visualize an office plan than this one (see Figure 4-15).

This spectacular flic is over 29MB, making it the largest in the *Walkthroughs & Flybys CD* collection. Contributing to its size is the fact that it was rendered so that each frame is dithered to smooth out the gradations between colors. Rendering flic files with dithering radically increases the data transfer rate required when they are played back because almost every pixel changes with every frame. Because the full 29MB KRAMER.FLI file would play unacceptably slowly from the CD, we have shrunk the animation to 1/4 of its size and named that file KRAMER2.FLI. If you would like to see the full-screen animation, you should copy KRAMER.FLI to your hard disk before viewing it with AAPLAY.

This animation was created by Jamie Clay with 3D Studio release 2.0 for inclusion in a video that was presented by Autodesk at "SIGGraph 1992." The rendering time averaged over 11 minutes per frame.

Simulating Explosions Without IPAS

Mike Morrison
ddd Graphics

MIS_STRK.FLI   1.2MB
EXP_SHIP.FLI   0.7MB
SUN_EXP.FLI   2.1MB

Figure 4-16 SUN_EXP.FLI

Mike Morrison has contributed three explosive FLI files to the *Walkthroughs & Flybys CD* collection. MIS_STRK.FLI shows the view from a missile as it rapidly approaches a battleship. The damage resulting from this attack is shown in EXP_SHIP.FLI by growing a series of translucent spheres the centers of which are near the point of impact. Realism is added by bits of debris flying in all directions.

The best of Mike's flics is SUN_EXP.FLI (see Figure 4-16), which shows the explosion of a sun deep in space. Note how the sun implodes slightly just after the impact of the missile. The use of a flat ring to create the illusion of a shock wave is particularly effective when the material used has a varying level of transparency. Be sure to notice the effect the shock wave has on the planet in the foreground as a small ring of fire seems to dance around its equator. The effect of the decaying fiery spheres is also created with an animated opacity map.

Mike's work shows off 3D Studio's ability to use a flic file to vary the degree of an object's transparency over time. In 3D Studio lingo, this is called using an animated opacity map. Mike's technique to create these starts with creating a Plasma cloud image in Fractint. The resulting GIF file is then loaded into Animator Pro and edited so that it can be *tiled*. By tiled we mean that when the map is placed next to itself, there are no visible seams where the edges meet. This image then becomes an animation with each pixel changing from its starting color to white over a period of so many frames. When this animated opacity map is then applied to an object during rendering, as more of the pixels of the map become white, more of the sphere becomes transparent.

Adding the Finishing Touches with Animator

Michael Mulholland
Student

CHESS.FLI   7.9MB

Figure 4-17 CHESS.FLI

Michael is currently studying computer graphics for his A levels in art with hopes of working in the computer graphics field full time upon completion of his studies. He runs 3D Studio on a loaded 486 with 16MB of RAM and a CD-ROM drive. His specialty is adding those lovely finishing touches with Animator Pro.

CHESS (Figure 4-17) is a flic that shows a game of Killer Chess being played from various angles. The rules of this strange variation are that if you can take a piece belonging to your opponent, then you must do so. Because Michael created CHESS when he had only 4MB of RAM in his machine, he learned a number of tricks for reducing rendering times. Because every scene has a static camera position with only one or two moving pieces at any given moment, Michael came up with a great technique for only rendering the pieces that move. First, he rendered all the stationary pieces, creating a GIF file of the scene. Then using the GIF file as the background, he rendered his animation with all the stationary pieces hidden, radically reducing the amount of computation necessary to create the final scene. Mike is sure that this valuable approach saved him days of rendering.

All the little subtle fades and tints that were added with Animator Pro really make this flic stand out. For example, notice how your eye is drawn to the piece just about to move by Michael's technique of causing its square to glow. The gradual fading away of the captured pieces was created by rendering two images, one with the captured piece and one without it, and then using the Animator Cross Fade option to merge them together. Many of the effects such as the snapping lightning bolts, the electrocution of the King (Figure 4-18), and the burning exhaust from the flying rooks are fine examples of this artist's skill at touching up 3-D animations with Animator.

There are three other fine examples of work by this artist. DRAGCAVE.FLI (0.4MB) and DRAGONB.FLI (1.3MB) show the creation of a realistic creature constructed of basic shapes. The snake skin material

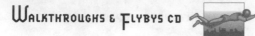

Figure 4-18 The electrocution from CHESS.FLI

from the 3D Studio World Builder CD-ROM was used to create the surface of this menacing viper. STARGLOB.FLI (1.6MB) is a nice circuit around a starship, but not quite in the same league as his other work.

Re-creating Lifelike Human Motion

Kenn Jordan
Screen Artists

ICL.FLI   7.5MB

Figure 4-19 ICL.FLI

The model for the running man in this flic was adapted from a set of photographs taken over 100 years ago by Eadweard Muybridge. This pioneer was the first person to use photography as a tool for analyzing the motion of living creatures. In his day there was no way to take several photographs in rapid succession with a single camera, so he used many cameras and focused instead on the triggering mechanisms. For example, he captured the image of a running horse by laying trip wires and cameras at regular intervals and running the horse over them.

ICL.FLI (Figure 4-19) started with a model of a human figure that was created by Gary Yost using a beta copy of Mannequin software. Kenn obtained this 3D Studio model by downloading it from CompuServe. Moving the limbs of the model in the 3D Studio Keyframer so that they corresponded to the positions in the Muybridge photographs was time consuming but not difficult. Small dark diamonds were added to the track to show that the figure is actually moving as opposed to running in place.

Robots and Mechanical Life

David Nielsen
Ketiv Technology

ROBOTRK.FLI   2.3MB

Figure 4-20 ROBOTRK.FLI

Some animations are classics. Although it is often difficult to predict the reaction of people to certain flics, others like ROBOTRK (Figure 4-20) are a sure hit every time. Is it our hatred of sitting in traffic or an envy of the power and solidity of the Big Rig that draws us to this wonderful animation? The star of this flic is a tractor trailer that sprouts legs and walks. David created this animation initially using Autoflix in EGA mode a couple of years before the release of Autodesk 3D Studio. The version we have included on the CD was rendered in Autoshade with the post-production work of adding titles and cross fades done in Animator. This animation won the 1990 CADDIE award.

More Robots and Mechanical Life

Greg St. George
Hanover Park, IL

KICKME.FLI   22.2MB

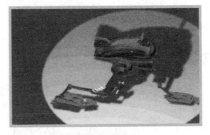

Figure 4-21 KICKME.FLI

This wonderful flic was the 1991 winner of the prestigious CADDIE award from Autodesk Inc. and CADalyst Magazine in the Independent Artist category. The following text is pulled directly from Greg's original background page.

"'Kick Me' [Figure 4-21] is an animation sequence inspired by a Nitto plastic model I built several years ago of a reconnaissance droid from sometime in the very near future that featured ceramic armor and artificial intelligence to gather information on enemy forces. This kit builds into a very believable version of this concept. Too believable, in fact. Therefore, I wanted to inject an element of humor into this efficient analytical android.

"My solution was to pose it in an animation sequence opening with the droid in a powered-down state. It 'wakes up' with the suspicion that something is amiss. A quick scan to the sides reveals nothing so it strides off in search of the cause of its discontent. The camera angle first follows and then flies underneath the droid to show the mechanical efficiency of its movement. Finally stopping, the droid again scans left and right as the camera circles in front of and then behind it. As the camera stabilizes at its rear, a sheet of ordinary notebook paper comes into view with the two words 'Kick Me' scrawled in big black letters. Fulfilling that imperative, another droid's leg swings in from off-camera and soundly sends the subject flying off into space. There it ends."

The only software used to create KICKME.FLI was Autodesk 3D Studio Version 1. The sequence took 31 hours and 22 minutes to render on an ALR 486/33 with 5MB RAM. The entire animation was created within the first three weeks of the artist's purchase of 3D Studio.

Greg is most proud of the juxtaposition of high-tech imagery with a low-tech practical joke. Be sure to notice the piece of cellophane tape holding the sign to the droid's backside as an example of his attention to detail.

Playing SuperVGA Flic Files (FLC)

The flics in this section are in the Animator Pro FLC format. Unfortunately, the Trilobyte PLAY program that we have chosen to play FLC files doesn't provide for any interactive selection. Instead Automenu will execute the PLAY viewer in script mode, playing each of the selected flics in turn. To get started from the Main Menu choose:

Autodesk 3D Studio Animations Menu, then choose
640x480 FLC Files

At this point, you will be faced with three choices:

1. View SuperVGA flics by Artist
2. Copy 75MB of FLC files to the hard disk and play
3. Play all SuperVGA FLCs from the CD

Selecting the first option will bring up a submenu that will let you see all of the SuperVGA flics created by a particular artist. Use the options from this submenu to find the movies described in the remainder of this section.

Choosing the second option will prompt you for a destination drive letter onto which to copy 75MB of FLC files. That drive will be examined for available disk space, a subdirectory will be created, and all of the relevant files will be copied into it. If you are using a CD-ROM drive with a 150K per second data transfer rate, this process should take about nine minutes. Once the files are copied, you will be asked to press any key to start the animations. To exit any of the PLAY scripts, press the (ESC) key and you will be returned to the control of the menu system.

Choosing the third option from this menu instructs PLAY to display each of the SuperVGA FLC files by loading them directly from the CD. A black screen will be displayed while PLAY loads the flics into memory one at a time.

Advanced Use of Texture and Opacity Maps

Ingo Neumann

Animation & Grafik

SPEAFIRE.FLC   13.9MB

Figure 4-22 SPEAFIRE.FLC

This monster of a flic was created by Ingo Neumann of Wiesbaden, Germany to promote the SPEA Fire board, a high-performance graphics acceleration card. It is a fine example of using texture and opacity mapping to produce an out-of-this-world effect. The animation opens by fading up to reveal black lines tracing the outline of the SPEA logo (see Figure 4-22). Once the logo is complete, fire burns away the outlined areas to reveal the red and white stripes of the SPEA logo. Fireworks appear and burst over the scene as the Fire logo glides in from below.

Here is how Ingo created the tracing lines of the logo. First a black and white flic file was created of four spheres each traversing the path of one of

Figure 4-23 Balls tracing the SPEA logo

the four letters, as seen in Figure 4-23. This flic was rendered from the front viewport so as not to be distorted by perspective. The motion of each of the spheres around its path was transformed into the tracing illusion by using the Animator Pro Trails effect with the nonzero clear option. The flic was then colored to be red and black before it was ready to be used as the main texture and opacity map for the scene.

The effect of the burning fire revealing the red and white stripes of the SPEA logo starts with a file on the 3D Studio World Builder CD-ROM called BURN2.FLC. This animation of burning fire slowly growing to cover the entire screen is used as an Animated Matte in the Animator Pro Join menu. As more of the fire covers the screen, more of the red and white stripes are revealed. The resultant flic is then texture mapped onto the SPEA logo before it is rendered again. The fireworks are added by overlaying another of the sample animations at the end using the Animator Pro Composite feature.

Another great SuperVGA flic created by this artist with 3D Studio is REFLCTS.FLC. And don't miss Ingo's fly-through of Crater Lake, CRATER.FLI, which is described in the next section.

In the Style of MC Escher

Simon Browne

ROOM.FLC   4.0MB
FISH.FLC   1.9MB
DOLPHIN.FLC   8.7MB
HEAD1.FLC   5.5MB

Figure 4-24 ROOM.FLC by Simon Browne

The animations ROOM (Figure 4-24) and FISH are Simon's way of paying homage to MC Escher whose work he greatly admires. As Simon is quick to point out, Escher once commented that he couldn't draw and that his skills were derived from meticulous planning in the use of geometry and perspective. This fascination with Escher's work colors the way Simon looks at projects. While he feels that using each aspect of 3D Studio is easy enough in isolation, pulling everything together requires a structured approach. For this reason he feels that his ability to plan his animations in advance is his strongest asset.

You will also enjoy watching two other animations by this artist. DOLPHIN is an 8.7MB file that was made purely for fun. Having seen these creatures flourishing in their natural habitat encouraged this attempt to re-create their world. HEAD1 is a 5.5MB representation of a Bell-type cyclic pitch controller for the rotor of a helicopter. The complex linkages exist to slow down the response of the main rotor to the point where human reaction times are adequate.

Creating the Haunting and Supernatural

Rob Stein III

Anigraf/x

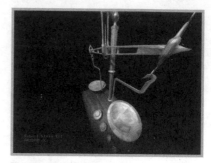

SCALE.FLC	1.3MB
SKULL.FLC	0.5MB
SWIM.FLC	2.1MB
CYCART_1.FLI	2.4MB
PLAYROOM.FLI	1.0MB

Figure 4-25 SCALE.FLC

Rob is a 3-D animator and traditional graphics artist who works free lance through his company Anigraf/x. Most of his time lately has been spent working with Trilobyte, the Oregon-based PC games creator whose titles are published under the Virgin Label. Currently their title "7th Guest" is enjoying enormous popularity, just as their Alice in Wonderland game did before it.

SCALE (Figure 4-25) is a beautiful animation that demonstrates extreme perspective. Be sure to notice the accuracy of the reflections in the dishes as they move up and down. Because all of the materials in this scene are in yellow and brown hues, there is no contouring in the colors whatsoever. This flic is a great example of just how photorealistic a 256-color animation can be if the range of colors is kept quite narrow. SWIM is a morphing experiment rendered against a backdrop of an image that won top honors in the Truevision 92 Awards. Skull is a very creepy animation of a shadow flowing endlessly over a human skull. Rob also has two standard VGA FLI files in the \FLIC\FLI directory that are outstanding. CYCART_1.FLI and PLAYROOM.FLI are both lead-in animations for an unfinished game called CYBERNET.

FLICS CREATED WITH NON-AUTODESK SOFTWARE

In this section we will present you with animations in the flic format that have been created with tools other than 3D Studio. We'll take a look at an animator who borrows heavily from traditional methods before flying through some landscapes created with VISTAPRO. You'll also get to see some animations created with the freeware raytracing program Persistence of Vision (POV-Ray).

Animation Using Stop-Motion and Pixillation

Tom Guthery IV
FLIX Productions

GUMBY.FLI   2.3MB
TOMBRAIN.FLI 1.5MB
BZOOM320.FLI 1.0MB

Stop-motion animation is a technique where a pliant model is moved in increments being filmed a frame at a time. *Pixillation* is a related technique where real humans are employed as the models from which accurate motion is derived. One of the best known pioneers of this technique was Willis O'Brien whose *King Kong* (1933) is in many respects unsurpassed today. His specially designed miniature sets and ability to combine footage of an animated model with live actors were the keys to his success. Stop-motion animation techniques, such as those used to make *King Kong*, translate well to the PC. Ray Harryhausen is also well known for his use of stop-motion animation in *Jason and the Argonauts* (1963).

Borrowing techniques that are decades old and applying them in a computer environment can yield very attractive results. Besides the amount of time saved by not having to create and render in a package such as 3D Studio, the fact that the model is a real object gives a very cinematic look to the result.

Animating an Articulated Model

To animate an articulated figure, the model is first posed in the desired position, a frame is grabbed, then the model is moved again, and another frame grabbed, etc. The technical means of accomplishing this is relatively easy compared to the "artistic" skills needed to move the model in a pleasing way. It helps to think of the object moving in slow motion as it is being positioned. Animating a human figure for your first attempt is probably not a very good idea, as humans are especially aware of how humans are supposed to move. A helpful aid for human figure animation is to shoot some video of a real human and then play it back a frame at a time for study. You'll be surprised at how "unnatural" human movement is when closely examined. If the subject of an articulated animation is not supposed to be realistic, you have a lot more latitude in how it should look.

Lighting

One of the most important factors in producing a nice image of the model is lighting. Use of a primary light in front of the model and a backlight to fill in the shadows should do nicely, but it is well worthwhile to experiment. Dramatic effects can be achieved by strategic use of lighting (which explains why it is a discipline with it's own cadre of film professionals). For a background, use black velvet cloth to absorb the light. This is particularly important so that more colors are free to be used for the model rather than being wasted displaying subtle shades of black. By restricting the number of colors used in the background to as few as possible, they can be easily replaced later with another color or image.

Hardware and Software

It is interesting to note that this stop-motion animation technique is not computationally intensive. Compared to the caliber of PC used to generate the 3D Studio animations in the previous section, the 16MHz 386SX used here is a child's toy. For video capture, a ComputerEyes/RT capture card and a home video camera were used. Software that comes with the capture board acquires the images which are then combined into a flic file using Animator Pro. Animator Pro is particularly useful for working with the captured images because it gives you the ability to combine several shots with cinematic-type tools like fades, dissolves, and wipes. Also the color reduction and palette optimization tools make it ideal for this kind of work.

Bringing Gumby to Life

The Gumby figure was created by Paul Smith, a gifted sculptor and movie effects wizard. He first sculpted the figure in clay, then cast a mold to make the final figure with foam latex. Inside the figure there is a wire armature that serves as a skeleton which is jointed to provide natural movement. Soldered to the bottom of the feet are two nuts, which allow the figure's feet to be bolted to a surface to provide stability while the figure is being manipulated (as in Figure 4-26). Figures can be constructed in clay but foam latex provides a very durable yet flexible skin.

The smoke effect used in the opening of GUMBY.FLI was created by blowing smoke in front of the lens of the camera with the ComputerEyes/RT capture card running in real-time mode. Placing the main light above created a dramatic effect helping to bring out the sculpted detail in the

Figure 4-26 Tom Guthery with Gumby

figure. The "magic wand" was a ruler with its side held to the camera's point of view. The colored sparkles were painted in later with Animator Pro, particular attention being given to having them loosely track with the wand. Each step of the zoom was done in single frame mode to provide precise control. Dollying the camera was avoided as it would have entered a jerkiness into the animation.

A great deal of concentration was required to remember which limb was going in what direction because several things were happening at once. The movement was done with no references to books, photos, or drawings.

The realism of Gumby's features in extreme close-up is testimony to Paul's sculpting ability. As you watch this flic, keep in mind that the head of the model is only one inch high. Tiny wires extend from the jaw so that the mouth can be manipulated into various positions. The mouth itself is so tiny that a small tool had to be used to pry it open. The tongue was made of several tiny pieces of clay sculpted to the desired shape. Small pieces are used at first, then bigger ones, to give the illusion that the tongue is coming out of the mouth, as can be seen in Figure 4-27. The color-matched clay was used for other purposes as well, such as closing the eyelids.

Two FLIs were dissolved using an Animator Pro transition to lead into the final section. Another camera zoom was deliberately avoided because one had been used before. Tom feels that generally it isn't a good idea to move the point of view constantly, unless you are trying to get a roller-

Figure 4-27 Close-up of Gumby's head

coaster effect. For the finale, real-time record mode was used to reveal the stage, back drop, and studio. The final shot with Tom in the frame shows the size of the articulated model.

GUMBY.FLI took about four hours to animate in front of the camera and another four hours to assemble in Animator Pro. Most of the Animator Pro time was spent cleaning up the background color that hadn't come out completely black.

BZOOM320.FLI

This FLI file of a rotating human brain, as shown in Figure 4-28, is an outtake from a recent project. The program was designed to be used by neurologists, so accuracy was a must. Creating a computer model of a brain would have taken forever using a 3-D program. The need for cut-away shots and views from many different angles further complicated the project. The problem was solved by purchasing an accurate model of the brain from a biological supply company and animating it with traditional stop-motion techniques.

Tom is also a gifted GRASP programmer. If you have young children, you will be particularly interested in Tom's Animated Words (AWORDS.EXE) educational software. You will find his work with GRASP located under the **Grasp Demos** Main Menu selection.

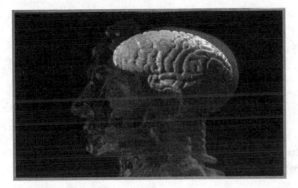

Figure 4-28 BZOOM320.FLI

Flybys Generated with VISTAPRO

There are a number of special-purpose 3-D programs for the PC that have varying degrees of popularity. One of the most interesting is John Hinkley's VISTAPRO which is published by Virtual Reality Laboratories. This program simulates the detail of 3-D landscapes by reading the Digital Elevation Model (DEM) files such as those published by the U.S. Geological Survey. When VISTAPRO reads in a DEM file, it creates a mesh of up to 131,000 polygons to represent the terrain. The user can add trees, rivers, and lakes to the model as well as adjusting various parameters such as the amount of haze or the height of the snow line. First, let's look at a really big flyby created by one of the European masters.

CRATER.FLI

Ingo Neumann
Animation & Grafik

CRATER.FLI   9.9MB

Figure 4-29 CRATER.FLI

Ingo is a very clever animator with extensive technical knowledge of computers and programming. Recognizing that one of the limitations of version of VISTAPRO was the necessity to render a single camera position at a time, he developed a way to generate VISTAPRO camera path scripts from within 3D Studio. As you can see in CRATER.FLI (Figure 4-29), the camera path is very smooth as it takes advantage of 3D Studio's ability to automatically bank a camera as it flies along a nonlinear path. Another thing to notice about this FLI is how smoothly the camera accelerates and decelerates.

The original FLC file was 32MB in size, having taken 6.5 hours to render at 640x480 resolution. The file was reduced to 320x200 resolution with the ANICONV program that comes with Autodesk Animator Pro.

CCDOBJCT.FLI

Jeff Alu

CCDOBJCT.FLI	0.2MB
CCDOBJC2.FLI	4.9MB
MSH.FLI	0.6MB
MONFLI.FLI	0.6MB

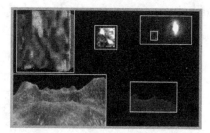

Figure 4-30 CCDOBJCT.FLI

Jeff has spent a great deal of time looking at the heavens in his former position with Jet Propulsion Labs. The 3-D terrain used for the flyby in CCDOBJC2.FLI comes from a "defect" he found in a CCD image of a galaxy. Normally defects in computer images are an annoyance; however, this one possessed a regularity and undulating pattern that Jeff thought would lend itself well to a 3-D animation. The file CCDOBJCT.FLI shows the progression of steps needed to bring this flyby to life.

The first image in the upper right of Figure 4-30 is that of the galaxy with the area of defect marked. This area is then enlarged to slightly reduce the variations of pixel intensity before importing the image into VISTAPRO where it is transformed into 3-D based upon pixel brightness. In other words, brighter pixels are given higher elevations, while darker pixels are given lower ones. A Martian orange color scheme is then applied to the scene, which results in the third image when rendered from above with VISTAPRO. The fourth image shows the view from within the 3-D terrain, while the fifth and final image is the first frame of the flyby.

CCDOBJC2 is the actual flyby. The complex banking camera path was created using the VISTAPRO Makepath Flight Director. This add-on utility facilitates not only the creation of a camera path, but also provides a previewing capability. Defining the camera path took about 10 minutes while rendering. CCDOBJC2.FLI took two hours on a 486. Be sure to check out MONFLI.FLI (a flight around the caldera of Olympus Mons on Mars) also created by Jeff Alu with VISTAPRO.

Animations Created with POV-Ray

The most popular raytracing program in the public domain at the moment is Persistence of Vision or POV-Ray for short. This immensely powerful application was created by a dedicated team of programmers and artists in the GO GRAPHDEV forum of CompuServe. Versions are available with full source code for the PC, Macintosh, and Amiga, with several other platforms currently under development. For more information on POV-Ray, see The Waite Group's *Ray Tracing Creations* by Drew Wells.

BLOB.FLC

Bill Pulver

BLOB.FLC   3.0MB

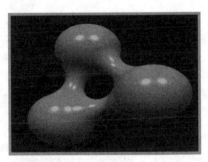

Figure 4-31 BLOB.FLC

BLOB.FLC (Figure 4-31) was created on an IBM-compatible, 80486DX/33-based machine running POV-Ray Version 1.0 as a background task under OS/2 2.0. Rendering all of the frames for the sequence "only took a little over a day." The effect of the spheres growing into each other was made by varying the "threshold" value of the "BLOB" primitive from 0 to 1. The color values for red and blue were also varied between 0 and 1, while green was held at 0. The values for the colors were varied in "opposite" directions. While red was varied from 1 down to 0, blue was varied from 0 up to 1. This caused the color to fade through the spectrum between full red to full blue. The batch file and image "source" include files were created by using the values generated by a modified version of CAMPATH.EXE by John Hammerton to vary the threshold and color values in even steps rather than the camera location values that the program was written to generate. The actual FLC file was created with DTA.EXE (Dave's Targa Animator) by David K. Mason using the "ping-pong" mode to create a symmetric animation. By symmetric we mean that only half of the total frames seen were actually generated, with the second half being a mirror image of the first.

LOWLOGO.FLI

Kirt Prchlik

Trik Graphics Corp

LOWLOGO.FLI   3.1MB

Figure 4-32 Screen shot of LOWLOGO.FLI

Kirt needed to produce an animated 3-D logo for a trade show display. Not having access to Autodesk 3D Studio, he set out to accomplish similar results with POV-Ray. Kirt's PC took over 40 hours of continuous computer time to generate the 150 unique views of the logo that were created by rotating the camera and light source in a circular path, a frame of which can be seen in Figure 4-32. The scripted lettering of the logo was created using TrueType fonts in PC Paintbrush. The various parts, including the transitional morph, were tied together with Autodesk Animator.

CHAPTER

DEMOS FOR THE PC

n this section, we will present the best multimedia demos we could find for the PC. Of the demo creation tools represented, GRASP by Paul Mace Software, Inc. dominates the collection. At the end of this chapter, we will present some interesting pieces created with Deluxe Paint Animation and Domark's Virtual Reality Toolkit. For more information on GRASP, see The Waite Group's *Multimedia Creations* by Phil Shaddock.

GRASP — GRAPHIC ANIMATION SYSTEM FOR PROFESSIONALS

There are literally dozens of programs available for creating demos on the PC, but none seem to be as popular with the demo pros as GRASP. In this section you will be introduced to this powerful authoring system and will be shown some examples of demonstrations that have been created with it.

Using this language is a bit like driving a race car. The uncomfortable interface is completely eclipsed by the joys of moving faster than you ever have before. However, this speed does not come without a price. To put it mildly, GRASP is not a system designed for the "drag-and-drop" crowd. Using this package requires a basic understanding of the way that the PC handles graphics, as well as an affinity for doing your computing at the command line. The good news is that people with relatively little programming experience are able to produce a basic presentation in just a matter of hours. Its basic function is to be the glue that wraps your sounds, movies, and interactivity together into a single bulletproof application.

Figure 5-1 The GRASP package

Why It's the Choice of the Pros

This program leads the pack because it is so incredibly fast compared to any of the competition. While it is possible to create interactive multimedia in a number of packages, few of them can boast the performance and flexibility of GRASP (Figure 5-1). Most DOS-based authoring systems (such as Storyboard Live! and VCN Concorde) push ease of use as their main selling point. Others (such as Dan Bricklin's Demo Program) focus on quick prototyping of user interfaces. Exciting newcomers (such as Tempra Show and PC Animate) have their own strengths, all jostling together to gain a market share in the rapidly expanding market for DOS-based multimedia.

GRASP's Niche

GRASP has successfully built its niche by concentrating on giving developers fast manipulation of graphics memory and extensive control of PC resources right down to the hardware level. No sacrifices are made for ease of use. Being able to send interrupts, write to ports, and POKE data into specific memory locations are the kinds of things that separate GRASP from the other packages on the market. There is no doubt that misusing these features will cause the PC to crash; but when speed is of the essence, this isn't such a great price to pay.

The other major aspect of GRASP that makes it so popular is its openness. Demo developers use literally dozens of programs in conjunction with this system. If you don't like the paint program or text editor that comes as part of GRASP, it is very easy to substitute another. Because the author, John Bridges, is dedicated to supporting industry standards, GRASP has the ability to run flic animations and display PCX or GIF images at runtime.

Features and Benefits of GRASP

- This interpreted programming language is optimized for manipulating graphics and, as a result, is much faster than any GUI-based system.

- It will convert or load at runtime static paint images in PCX or GIF format or movies in the Autodesk FLI and FLC formats.

- GRASP supports all text and graphics modes up to 1024x768x256 colors.

- It offers the PICTOR paint program for creating images.

- The GDFF differential compiler assembles ranges of pictures into a stream of their differences for high-speed differential animation. Unlike Autodesk flics, GRASP differentials can be played backwards.

- The GLIB and GLEXE utilities pack all of your files together into a single encrypted EXE file, so your application can be more easily moved to other machines.

- The Image Tools and Art Tools utilities algorithmically manipulate images, allowing you to stretch, warp, and even morph from one bitmap to another.

- Most importantly, GRASP gives the developer complete control of the lowest level of the PC through interrupt calls and the ability to read from and write to ports. This functionality gives you the flexibility to write your own drivers for such diverse peripherals as barcode readers, touch screens, and other types of data acquisition equipment.

What the Code Looks Like

To create a demo in GRASP, you must first decide which video mode you want to use and create your image accordingly. Generally, you have to initialize the video mode, set the palette for your image, and then display it. Here is a quick GRASP listing of how that would be done in GRASP code. The text after the semicolons are comments.

LISTING 5-1 SAMPLE GRASP CODE TO DISPLAY A GIF PICTURE.

```
video s                 ;Set 640x480x256 color video mode
pload walkthru.gif 1    ;Load a GIF file into picture buffer 1
palette 1               ;Change the current palette to that of the picture
pfade 12 1              ;Bring buffer one to the screen with fade 12
pfree 1                 ;Release the buffer and reclaim its memory
waitkey                 ;Wait for a key to be pressed.
```

To learn more about actually creating demos with GRASP, get *Multimedia Creations* from The Waite Group by Phil Shaddock.

GRASP-Based Demos

Here are the best corporate presentations we could find. Frequently they contain elements that present a company product. Most have no sound to help grab the user's attention but rely instead upon flashy graphics and concise copy to convey their messages. Many use interactivity to let you select a branch in the story or answer a quiz. Others spit out digitized sound to highlight certain points. You'll find a floppy disk-based publication, a medical seminar, and a kiosk application, as well as many other interesting and novel uses of multimedia.

Instructions for Running These Demos

The description of every demo listed in this chapter is preceded by a six-line set of vital statistics. These are

1. The company that created the demo.
2. The title under which it is referenced in the Menu System.
3. The name of the person who contributed the demo to the *Walkthroughs & Flybys CD* collection.
4. The DOS file name and path locating the demo on the CD.
5. Its size in megabytes.
6. The level of graphics required to run it.

To run a demo described in this chapter, first select **Demos Created with GRASP** from the Main Menu. You will be presented with a submenu that lists four ranges of the alphabet. Under each of these options you will find other menus for each demo creation company.

For example, if you want to run **DiscNews Volume 2** by Systemax Computer Graphics, choose option number 4. From that list, choose **DiscNews Volume 2, May 1992** to start this demo. Unless otherwise noted, press (ESC) to exit any of the demos in this section. Control will be returned to the menu system upon exiting.

The Six-Step Demo Creation Process

Company:	Systemax Computer Graphics
Title:	DiscNews Volume 2, May 1992
Contributor:	Tom Hudock
Path:	\DEMOS\SYSTEMAX\DNEWS002.EXE
Size:	1.2MB
Graphics:	EGA

Figure 5-2 DiscNews main menu

DiscNews is a floppy-based company newsletter put out every few months by Tom Hudock and his team. As the opening claims, Systemax creates professional demo disks. After you see the first few seconds of **DiscNews Issue 2**, you'll know that this boast isn't made idly. Their sense of screen design, sense of color composition, and programming skills are as good, if not better, than any of the teams whose work you will find on *Walkthroughs & Flybys CD*.

While publications on floppy disk aren't exactly a new idea, this effort by Systemax offers some nice twists. As you can see in Figure 5-2, the bold and bright screen layout and audible menu selections are certainly novel. Notice how the buttons for the interface are big, and noncomputer-like. While **DiscNews** certainly has a brilliant design, what really stands out is the content. Every article is relevant to the demo industry and advances in the area of multimedia. Of these articles, the most interesting is the "Systemax Six Step Demo Design Process" which you can start by selecting menu option F from within **DiscNews**.

Systemax has worked out a formula for structuring client contact to streamline the demo creation process. The technique involves the client at every step from the formulation of the original ideas to the delivery of the finished demo.

1. To fully understand the intended uses of the demo, Systemax uses a "Demo Disk Checklist" to guide consultations with the client. A detailed cost and time proposal is prepared based upon the information gathered. The screen for step one is shown in Figure 5-3.

2. To give the client an idea of the proposed approach, an initial outline is prepared with the client that describes the topics and features to be covered. Part of this outline is a storyboard composed of rough sketches of the proposed screens (all demos begin with a storyboard).

3. A text script is prepared that details copy, screen transitions, and proposed animation sequences. The goal of the script is to finalize the wording to ensure that the correct message is being conveyed.

4. Prototype screens are prepared that demonstrate the proposed layout, use of color, and typography. Armed with the script and prototype screens, the client is given one last opportunity to make significant changes.

5. All screens, copy, and animation sequences are assembled into a working demo which is presented to the client. Given the extensive client contact at each previous stage of the process, any changes made in step five are usually minor.

6. The completed demonstration and an installation routine are delivered accompanied by a post demo script. This document reflects any deviations from the original proposal and also provides technical and troubleshooting information.

Figure 5-3 The 6-step demo creation process from Systemax

To see the results of this process in action, choose any of their other demos. Systemax is extremely proud of the LaserMaster demo with its custom anti-aliased fonts.

Hold an Event on a Disk

Company: Enlighten
Title: Software Publishing Event on a Disk
Contributor: Steve Glauberman
Path: \DEMOS\ENLIGHTE\SPCEVENT.EXE
Size: 1.7MB
Graphics: EGA

Figure 5-4 SPCEVENT.EXE

Few demo companies are as large and successful as Steve Glauberman's Enlighten, whose specialty is producing software demonstrations. On the CD, you will find work the company has done for Software Publishing Corporation and Computer Associates. Each demo has been packed into a single EXE file so that it can be moved easily from machine to machine. All of these demos feature brilliant illustration, concise and informative copywriting, as well as excellent technical direction.

One of the most novel and entertaining of the Enlighten collection has to be the SPC Event on a Disk. This demo transports you to a function being hosted by Fred Gibbons, the Chairman of Software Publishing Corporation. While it is all tongue in cheek and features some pretty funny jokes, the demo is also informative. Half of it is devoted to a simulated hands-on demonstration of Harvard Graphics by the two product managers.

We open to a red carpet being rolled toward us by a curbside valet, as shown in Figure 5-4. There are illustrated figures standing on the sidewalk. One of them comments via a speech bubble that the red carpet must be for someone really important. This opening is typical of Enlighten's *focus on the viewer*. After some chitchat, we're ushered through a beautifully illustrated lobby and into a ballroom. After a moment, the lights dim and we find ourselves attending a product briefing that includes a hands-on demo of Harvard Graphics. The demo concludes with testimonials from a panel of satisfied expert users. This unique demo is loaded with breathtaking

Figure 5-5 The ballroom from SPCEVENT.EXE

illustrations (see Figure 5-5) and is generally a pleasure to watch. The artists at Enlighten are true masters of PC illustration, making the most of the limited colors and resolution of the now obsolete EGA.

For a more recent example of work from this group, don't miss **Enlighten's 1992 Christmas Card**. This VGA 640x480x16 demo will give you some new ideas for what to do with that horrible leftover Christmas fruitcake. You'll be rolling with laughter as cartoon characters attempt to dispose of this delicacy by using it as a hockey puck, scrub brush, and plant pot. The control of digitized sound in this demo is excellent.

Great Color Reduction to the EGA Palette

Company: Griffin Studios
Title: Puzzled by Promotion
Contributor: Bryan Saint Germain
Path: \DEMOS\GRIFFIN\PUZZLE.EXE
Size: Size 1.2MB
Graphics: Graphics: EGA

Figure 5-6 PUZZLE.EXE—The chicklets game

PUZZLE.EXE is a short promotional piece made with GRASP that is quite effective in showing the power of disk-based promotion to stand out in a crowd. The three things that should be noted about this demo are the concise message, the novelty of a game, and most importantly, the outstanding use of color. Let's briefly cover the first two points before moving on to color.

The message of this demo is that promotions on disk are effective. While the piece is certainly an ad for the services of Griffin Studios, it takes a broader view by presenting a nice summary of the features, benefits, and popular uses of PC-based marketing. Using the PC to sell products is still a new idea in some quarters and Griffin presents the concepts well. If the user pauses long enough after choosing a particular feature, the next one comes up automatically.

This demo is unique in the *Walkthroughs & Flybys CD* collection because it comes with a puzzle for you to try to solve (see Figure 5-6). This variation on the chicklets game shows off the speed and flexibility of GRASP. Short of writing this application in a compiled language like Pascal or C, it would be very difficult to create such a responsive interactive application.

The designer of this demo went to a great deal of trouble to produce the best possible graphics within the limitations of the 16 colors of the EGA. What makes the images look so good is not just his skill but also his knowledge of the tools. When looking at the bright, vibrant illustration of the first screen, which is shown in Figure 5-7, it seems highly unlikely that only the 16 colors of the EGA are being used.

Figure 5-7 Notice the fine color reduction in this opening image

Tip: Professional image processing programs, such as Aldus Photostyler which was used here, are able to algorithmically blend colors together to give the illusion of more color depth. Using a process commonly known as Floyd Steinberg dithering, it is quite easy to convert an image with say 256 colors down to 16 colors. Here is how the process works. First the program has to choose which palette of 16 colors would best describe the image at the lower color depth. By counting the number of pixels of each of the colors in the image, the most numerous 16 are chosen. Next, conversion of the 256-color image begins one pixel at a time with the program processing each scan line in turn. For every pixel that the program plots in the mode with the fewer colors, it records just how much difference, or error, there is between the color of the dot in the 256-color image and the closest color in the palette. In deciding which color to plot any particular dot of the image, the program considers the degree of error of a number of the surrounding dots. Because this technique works by spreading the error around, it is also commonly referred to as an error-distributed dither. There are a number of different variations on this algorithm that weight the error of neighboring dots differently. To get the best results, sometimes it is necessary to try a few different algorithms.

If you would like an example of what error-distributed dithering can do to bring a photograph down to the optimal 256 colors, run the **Victor Demo** you will find in the **Interactive Media Solutions** menu.

Make Them Chuckle, Nothing Sells Better

Company: Houston Graphics
Title: Demo for Borland's Sidekick II
Contributor: Duke Houston
Path: \DEMOS\HOUSTON\SK2DEMO.EXE
Size: 0.5MB
Graphics: EGA

Figure 5-8 Opening street scene from SK2DEMO.EXE

Houston graphics emphasizes communication in their projects. Quality design, illustration, and animation may be the body of the piece, but a clearly delivered message is its soul. All of the design work is dedicated to delivering the message that the client requires. Let's take a look at the first of the Houston Graphics demos on the CD.

The opening screen shown in Figure 5-8 shows a western prairie town. When three different gunfighters each want to challenge the sheriff to draw at the same time, he knows it's time to get organized. And what does every busy sheriff need? Sidekick II of course. After this silly opening we are led through a tour of Sidekick's features and benefits before the program repeats.

Tip: Duke's favorite painting program is Deluxe Paint II Enhanced (DP2E) from Electronic Arts. One of the nicest features of this program is its perspective tool which will warp a bitmap to a plane in 3-D while providing a high degree of anti-aliasing. This tool was used to create the dramatic opening street scene of the western town. While other popular paint programs have similar "2-1/2 D" capabilities, only DP2E will anti-alias a bitmap using the existing palette.

Tip: Duke finds that making a 16-color palette come alive is perhaps the most challenging aspect of creating animation for mass distribution. Color reduction algorithms, no matter how good, make purely mechanical decisions. Comparing an algorithmically generated palette with where an image starts to lose integrity is for Duke the key to producing a better image in 16 colors. Adjusting the colors of an algorithmically generated palette manually to create a custom lookup table always produces better results than any of the default settings he has tried.

A Monochromatic Demo for a Laptop

Company: Houston Graphics
Title: Everex Carrier SL/25 Demo
Contributor: Duke Houston
Path: \DEMOS\HOUSTON\SL25DEMO.EXE
Size: 1.8MB
Graphics: VGA

Figure 5-9 SL25DEMO.EXE

SL25DEMO.EXE for Everex, as seen in Figure 5-9, was created especially for the LCD display of the Everex Carrier SL/25. You will enjoy the 3-D modeling and animation that was created using Infini-D on a Macintosh before being ported to the PC. Stop-action photography was used to get the fluid motion of the figures, each frame having been laboriously scanned by hand. The quality of this demo just goes to prove that there is no substitute for hard work.

A Medical Application to Inform and Document Patient Consent

Company: Medical Multimedia Group
Title: Patient's Guide to Lower Back Pain
Contributor: Randale Sechrest, MD
Path: \DEMOS\MEDICALM\BACK.EXE
Size: 2MB of graphics
Graphics: VGA

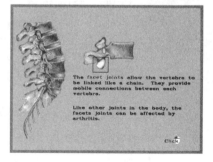

Figure 5-10 BACK.EXE

BACK.EXE is an interactive application that explains the causes of lower back pain in a layperson's terms. By using animated medical illustrations and digitized images as visual aids, the complicated concepts of degenerative disk disease are presented visually. Two sample screens from BACK.EXE are shown in Figures 5-10 and 5-11. This assists the patient in understanding not only his condition, but also the proposed treatment in a

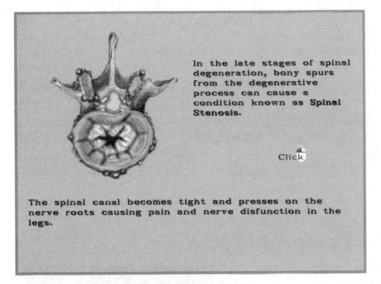

In the late stages of spinal degeneration, bony spurs from the degenerative process can cause a condition known as **Spinal Stenosis.**

Click

The spinal canal becomes tight and presses on the nerve roots causing pain and nerve disfunction in the legs.

Figure 5-11 Another screen from BACK.EXE

way that is interesting and self-paced. By presenting the material in a relatively linear fashion, as opposed to a "hypertext" organization, the information is conveyed systematically, enhancing the retention of those new to the topic.

This program is used as follows. After identifying the reason for a patient's visit and performing a physical examination, the problem is briefly discussed and a suggestion is made that the patient view the computer-based education program. The program is run on a PC which has been set up in an area of Dr. Sechrest's office specially devoted to patient education with all the explanatory pamphlets and models on hand. Following completion of the program, a more in-depth discussion of the patient's condition is possible because the physician can refer back to concepts presented in the presentation. The questions asked by the patient are more relevant because he has had an opportunity to become familiar with the material. To quote Dr. Sechrest, "The computer graphics allow both the physician and patient to have the same frame of reference instead of the patient trying to ascertain from his frame of reference what the doctor is trying to convey verbally."

If patients later come to surgery, they are asked to view the program again. At the end of the presentation, the patient is asked to complete the PC-based quiz which tests his understanding. If the patient receives a passing score on the quiz, *it demonstrates that he has a deep enough understanding of his condition to be able to consent to the surgical procedures.*

The results of the quiz can be printed and included in the patient's file documenting his informed consent. A failing score on the quiz indicates that more time needs to be spent educating the patient.

Both the doctor and the patient benefit from this marvelous use of multimedia. The doctor is saved from repeatedly explaining the same material in a complete and enthusiastic manner several times in a single day. Certainly, his time is much better spent answering questions after the patient already has some understanding of the material. The major benefit to the patient is derived from the power of interactive PC graphics to help convey the complicated material visually and in an interactive, self-paced manner.

Playing Graphics in Sync with CD Audio

Company:	Screen Artists Ltd.
Title:	The ICL 92 Collection
Contributor:	Phil Shatz
Path:	\DEMOS\SARTISTS
Size:	28MB of graphics & 5:20 seconds of CD Audio
Graphics:	SuperVGA (640x480x256)
Music:	The Multimedia Music Company

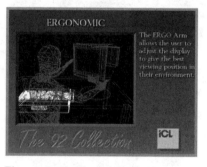

Figure 5-12 The 92 Collection

Your PC's CD-ROM drive can play audio CDs with the proper software; however, an audio CD player cannot access the data on a computer CD-ROM. Playing CD audio and accessing data from a CD-ROM are two completely different modes of operation that your drive is unable to perform concurrently. Because of this limitation, many CD-ROMs use audio cards like the Sound Blaster to play back digitized (VOC or WAV) and sequenced (CMF or MID) audio simultaneously with graphics. The approach most products take is to load the sound into memory and play it in a repeating loop while streaming the graphics from disk. This is how the first demo in *Walkthroughs & Flybys CD*, the BIGDEMO, is done. The music is quite repetitive and, occasionally, the graphics don't play smoothly due to the data transfer bottleneck of the CD-ROM.

The problem we faced on this project was that GRASP (or any other DOS-based authoring package for that matter) was unable to sustain playback of high fidelity sound simultaneously with SuperVGA 640x480 flic animations, such as the one shown in Figure 5-12. A full-length, continual soundtrack set to the graphics was a requirement for this demo, so we decided to take the route of laying the music and the GRASP demo both down on the CD. An installation program first copies the graphics to the hard disk. The GRASP program then begins playing the audio soundtrack as it plays the graphics. This approach offered the following advantages:

- Optimal sound quality with no costs in machine resources. Playing CD audio requires no CPU time at all, allowing the graphics to play simultaneously at full speed.

- Unlimited disk space for the animation files was available because a five minute soundtrack would only take up 50MB of the total 660MB available.

- The problem of transporting a large volume of data around on floppy disks was eliminated by the use of CD-ROM as the distribution medium.

The biggest disadvantage to this approach was that the target machines needed to play this demo frequently didn't have sufficient free disk space to hold all of the graphics. Another negative was the added cost of $2,500 to produce 50 copies of the CD.

Once all of the graphics were completed, we recorded the demo playing on a PC of the same speed as that of the target machine with a cheap video camera. The composers of the soundtrack, The Multimedia Music Company, added a SMPTE time code to this VHS tape so that they could use it as a timing master for their composition. In order to keep the demo in sync with the soundtrack, we established a dozen or so places *where the graphics would wait for the audio to catch up*. As the diagram in Figure 5-13 shows, at each of these points in the demo, we execute a small external program that repeatedly polls the CD-ROM driver until a particular point in time is reached. When audio has been playing long enough to reach that point, the external program terminates and the graphics continue. The amount of time that has elapsed since the start of playing a CD audio track can be obtained rather easily by calling a DOS interrupt.

The 92 Collection demo was a tremendous success for both Screen Artists and ICL. The impact of the high fidelity soundtrack in this

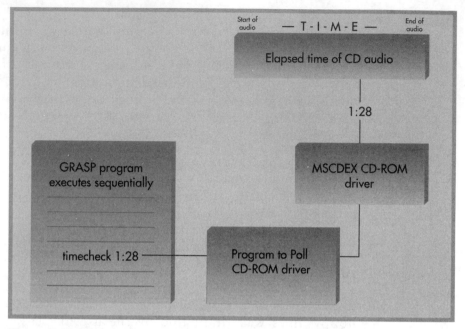

Figure 5-13 The graphics wait for the audio before proceeding

presentation more than made up for the added expense of the CD mastering and replication charges. Provided that you can assume a relatively large amount of free space on the target machine, this approach does have considerable merit.

What's a Kiosk?

Frequently these days we find computers standing alone in public places offering some type of information. This particular type of multimedia application is known as a *kiosk*. Touchscreens are generally more popular input devices than keyboards and mice, which tend to break or get clogged up with dirt. Kiosks are also usually set into a rugged exterior to stand the abuses inherent in unattended operation. Often times these systems will have a modem installed so that they can be updated from a remote location. Let's take a look at a sample kiosk application from Silver Tongue Software.

Peapod — A Kiosk Application

Company: Silver Tongue Software

Title: The Peapod Home Delivery Service

Contributor: Charles Jameson

Path: \DEMOS\SILVER_T\PEAPOD.EXE

Size: 6.2MB

Graphics: SuperVGA (640x480x256)

To Exit: (ALT)-(E)

Figure 5-14 PEAPOD.EXE

Silver Tongue Software has developed a system to promote a home shopping service called Peapod. The goal of the project was to communicate the benefits of shopping from home and having the goods personally delivered while not intimidating grocery store customers unfamiliar with computers. In addition to the SuperVGA kiosk application, a standard VGA demonstration was developed to be used as marketing collateral. The main advantage of having a standard VGA version was being able to distribute a model of Peapod without requiring any of the hassles associated with running actual software.

The structure of the kiosk and the demonstration floppy are identical and consist of two parts. Most of the time the kiosk is in "attract" mode (i.e., a short looping sequence that describes what Peapod is and how it works). This is done with three photographs showing the customer's order being placed, the goods being selected at the shop and, finally, their delivery to the home. For continuity, a bouncing "pea" icon leads the way from screen to screen, as can be seen in Figure 5-14. At any time the loop can be interrupted, taking the user to a menu.

The user interface for the menu is extremely simple, as seen in Figure 5-15. Selections can be made by moving the highlighted bar with the arrow keys and pressing (ENTER). Repeatedly pressing the (SPACEBAR) will also lead a viewer through the entire presentation. Each menu choice starts a segment that describes one of the benefits of Peapod. Actual screens from the system are shown to make the computer system credible, but these take second place to stressing the benefits and showing the people involved.

103

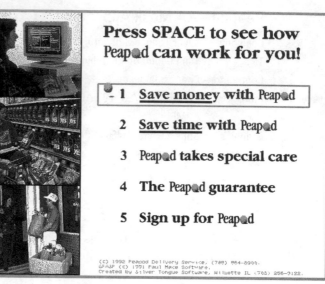

Figure 5-15 The PEAPOD menu

Tip: The bouncing pea in the introduction section and the shrunken version used as the menu selection pointer were created as an animated cel in Animator Pro. An Optics effect was used to move this cel along a path with care being taken that the pea was at the bottom of a hop when it changed from moving to bouncing in place. The interactivity of the menu screen, which is shown in Figure 5-15, was created with two GRASP differential files: one for the small pea and the other for the menu text. Moving the menu selection bar by pressing an arrow key causes the area of the bouncing pea to be cleared before a single frame of the menu differential is put to the screen. Unlike Animator flic differentials, GRASP DFFs are bidirectional. If the user presses the ⊕ key, the previous frame of the differential is put to screen. If the first image of the differential is currently being displayed, then pressing the ⊕ key brings up the last image in the sequence, that is, the one with the bottom menu selection highlighted. Since nothing moves over the photographs along the left side of the screen, the base picture is completely unaffected by the operation of the menu.

RealSound from the PC Speaker

Company: Interactive Media Solutions

Title: The IIT Math Coprocessor Demo

Contributor: Jason Gibbs

Path: \DEMOS\IMS\IIT\IIT.EXE

Size: 1.2MB

Graphics: VGA

Figure 5-16 Caveman from IIT.EXE

Because IMS is the official European distributor for GRASP, you would expect their work to be good. We are going to look at two examples of their work close up starting with the most humorous one.

This demonstration, a screen from which can be seen in Figure 5-16, developed for Integrated Information Technology Europe's Math Coprocessor shows an efficient use of digitized sound. The sound clips used in this demo are all quite short, but they are very effective in the way they punctuate certain points. Because GRASP has quite sophisticated digitized sound capabilities, it is possible to detect and play audio through not just the PC Speaker but also a Sound Blaster, Covox Speech Thing, or Adlib card. A GRASP user who wants to add digitized audio to his presentation just needs to load the small program file called SOUNDPC.GRP into memory before being able to address the sound driver. (Phil Shaddock covers this topic extensively in his Waite Group Press book *Multimedia Creations*. Be sure to run **Enlighten's 1992 Christmas Card** for another fine example of using digitized sound from within GRASP.)

As you can see from the opening screen shown in Figure 5-17, this demo runs in any of the 10 languages denoted by the flags. There is also an icon in the corner indicating whether or not you want sound enabled. Choose Ⓕ for English to begin. The opening shot is a funny drawing of a caveman in agony as his PC flashes WAIT in red. We can hear groans of despair coming from the PC speaker as the copy on the screen appears: "Do you feel that your PC is so slow that it must be a prehistoric relic?" The answer to the caveman's dilemma appears on the screen in the form of an illustration of the coprocessor's packaging that is accompanied by the blaring of trumpets. Other uses of digitized sound worth noting are the applause, section breaks, and audible responses to selections made during a question and answer session.

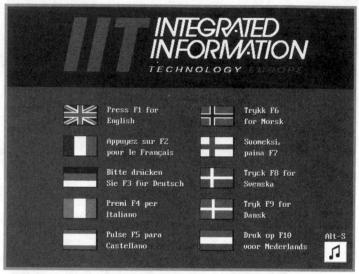

Figure 5-17 IIT screen with flags

Tip: One last thing to notice about this demo is the beautiful way in which the anti-aliased text is used. IMS has developed GRASP routines to generate smooth text on the fly during the running of the demo. Their trick is to write each line of text into an off-screen buffer using three different fonts. Each character in each of the three fonts provides a different level of aliasing. To do this in GRASP, each character must have the same maximum pixel width in each of the three fonts so the characters will be perfectly aligned when they are typed to screen.

Cartoons Drawn in Color on the PC

Company:	Interactive Media Solutions
Title:	The OAG Flight Disk
Contributor:	Jason Gibbs
Path:	\DEMOS\IMS\OAG\OAG.EXE
Size:	0.7MB
Graphics:	VGA

Figure 5-18 The Official Airlines Guide demo

"Bahrain and Back or Bust" would be a good way to describe this demo that tells the story of a stressed-out business traveler looking for flights at the last minute. The OAG Flight Disk comes to the rescue by giving the traveler the freedom to book flights from his PC.

Even though the cartoons are crude (Figure 5-18), the storyline is well written and holds our attention. The client was smart enough to tell a story the viewer could relate to rather than trying to squeeze in every feature and benefit one after another. Demos are becoming common enough now that the unique ones will stand out and be remembered.

From a technical standpoint, again notice the high level of configurability in the demos from IMS. The story can be told in one of five languages from the standpoint of either the traveler or the secretary. Also notice the lovely anti-aliased fonts that IMS generates on the fly as the demo is running. While this effect works well, it can significantly degrade performance when run on slower PCs.

Using Grayscaled Cartoons

Company: Screen Artists Ltd. /

                           Quad Production Company

Title: Toshiba T2000 Demo

Contributor: Andy Dean

Path: \DEMOS\SARTISTS\T2000.EXE

Size: 2.7MB

Graphics: VGA

Figure 5-19 Toshiba T2000

The artwork for the **Toshiba T2000 Demo,** samples of which can be seen in Figures 5-19 and 5-20, was drawn in pencil by John Richardson of Middlesborough, U.K. before being scanned in at 16 shades of gray. You can see how much more smoothly the gradations appear when the images are drawn by hand and then scanned as opposed to having been created originally on the PC.

The director of this demo, Andy Dean of the Quad Production Company in Cambridge, U.K. had a very exact idea of what he wanted. In addition to providing all of the artwork ready for scanning, he also had all of the text in English and German to accompany it. This demo is fun to watch as much for its strong storyline as anything else. Let's watch this man down on his luck find salvation through Toshiba portable computers.

This demo opens with a sequence in which letters spelling the word "Toshiba" grow as the company slogan "In Touch with Tomorrow" fades in.

Figure 5-20 Toshiba T2000

By using Animator Pro's Optics panel, this zooming effect on the letters was created in very little time. Actually, the process of converting each of the individual images for this sequence down to 16 colors and building a GRASP differential to play them back was much more time consuming than the actual creation of the effect in Animator Pro. With a shift of all the colors in the palette to bright white, we begin the demo proper.

The specification for the T2000 demo was to provide maximum editability of all the textual information for the purpose of easing the task of creating translations. In order to accommodate the varying number of lines that the demo text would require, a routine was written that would size the height of the text box and draw the bevels accordingly. On a slow PC, you will notice that the text is painted with two visible passes — the black first and then the gray aliasing color. This base routine is used to display the text on each of the 15 frames' different scanned images.

Demos Created with Other Tools

Of the many products available for creating demos on the PC, two of the most interesting are Domark's VR Studio and Deluxe Paint Animation from Electronic Arts. These two programs couldn't be more different. VR Studio shines in the immediate redisplay of a 3-D perspective when the user changes his view interactively. While Deluxe Paint Animation is very similar in functionality to Autodesk's Animator program, it features an interface that is much easier for artists to master.

Domark's VR Studio

Company:	Charles Carr
Title:	3D House
Contributor:	Charles Carr
Path:	\DEMOS\CARR\3DHOUSE.BAT
Size:	0.2MB
Graphics:	VGA
To Start:	Choose **3D House by Charles Carr** from the **Miscellaneous Demos Menu**.
To Quit:	Press (CTRL)-(ESC)

Figure 5-21 3D House

This unique demo will let us wander around the house and grounds of Charles Carr, the creator of this demo. This is all possible thanks to the amazing Virtual Reality Studio program from Domark. The interface is quite straightforward and fun to use. By clicking your mouse on one of the six main arrows, you can move or swivel your view in a number of different directions. The two smaller vertical arrows that are above and below the eyeball will move your view up and down. Black areas, such as the garage doorway in Figure 5-21, signify doors into other viewing areas. Double-clicking on one of these doors will move you into that new area.

One restriction of VR Studio is that only 60 objects are allowed per viewing area. This is why the living room is rather lacking in detail compared to smaller areas like the bedrooms. For example, since the stairway takes up 13 of the 60 available objects, Charles debated whether to use a symbolic ramp to free up more objects with which he could create more detail. Another challenge when building virtual worlds with this system is that there is no facility for creating rounded objects. To create the heart you will find on the headboard in one of the bedrooms, Charles placed two five-sided polygons next to each other.

This tour of the Carr residence took about 200 hours to create, but that figure includes the learning curve. Mr. Carr comments that using VR Studio gives you the feeling that you are creating something in the physical sense. One of the nicest things about Virtual Reality Studio is its incredibly low price of $100. For ordering information you can contact either their U.S. or U.K. office, both of which are listed in Appendix C, *Sources*.

Deluxe Paint Animation

Company:	The Artwork Exchange
Title:	Watch This Space & Wormville
Contributor:	Pat Nessling
Path:	Wormville & Watch This Space
Size:	6.0MB
Graphics:	VGA
To Start:	Choose **The Artwork Exchange** from the **Miscellaneous Demos Menu**.
To Quit:	Press (ESC)

Figure 5-22 The smiling woman from Watch This Space

Pat Nessling is an experienced illustrator of children's books with inks and watercolors who recently started drawing on the PC. At present, she spends about half of her time drawing in each of these two mediums. Her style tends toward the romantic and mystical with the ability to apply realism. People and scenes are her strong point as well as painting ethnic groups. Pat is one of the artists in "The Artwork Exchange," a U.K.-based group of established artists and illustrators who cover a wide variety of styles.

In her piece Wormville, Pat used the AnimBrush feature of Deluxe Paint Animation to apply motion to her figures of people and dragons. Because an AnimBrush is a series frames that can be transparently painted over complex backgrounds, it was the perfect tool for creating the character animation of this piece. "Watch This Space" was also created completely in Deluxe Paint Animation and makes heavy use of gradated fills to achieve smooth textures. Pat is especially proud of the way the woman smiles at the end of this piece, as you can see in Figure 5-22.

Demos Created with Proprietary Software

In this section, we will look at a demo created with a program that isn't available to the general public. The demo system used below has some advantages over GRASP, particularly with regard to ease of use.

While having complete control over all aspects of a particular development environment may appear to be ideal, there are some serious disadvantages to rolling your own. First, the costs of developing reliable, high-performance graphics software are substantial. If the entire cost of a demo development system must be borne by the single group that uses them, then those costs must be passed on to the client. As with any software package, enhancement is generally dependent upon the willingness and reliability of a single programmer. If that person decides, for whatever reason, to leave the demo development group, then they could find themselves being seriously stuck.

The benefits of using a proprietary system for creating demos are, however, quite significant. Adding a particular feature is just a matter of enhancing one's program rather than relying on GRASP. The most important reason to use other tools probably has to do with the awkwardness of the GRASP interface. If proprietary tools offer an easier and quicker way for users to assemble their presentations, then the time savings and increased productivity alone justify their use.

Marketing Consumer Electronics Equipment

Company:	Animated Systems & Design
Title:	Pioneer Home Theater Demo
Contributor:	Rae Callender
Path:	\DEMOS\ASDI\PIODEMO.EXE
Size:	2.1MB
Graphics:	EGA
To Start:	Choose **Pioneer Home Theater** from the **Miscellaneous Demos Menu**.
To Quit:	Press (ESC)

Figure 5-23 PIONEER.EXE

This demonstration disk was created to promote the Pioneer Home Theater concept. The purpose of the demo is not just for fulfillment of direct mail and ad response, but also to be run on dedicated machines at the point of purchase. Animated Systems claims that this is the first time a demo disk has been used to market consumer electronics, marking the penetration of multimedia into a new niche.

This demo is fun to watch! The Cool Cat and Cool Guide characters come to life through their silly jokes and humorous antics to guide you through the many branches of this demo. Keeping in mind that so many interactive demo disks fail to hold the user's attention regardless of how technically brilliant their design, Animated Systems focused on humor. Stunning graphics (see Figure 5-23) and animation were also used to hammer home one of Pioneer's main marketing messages — you don't just watch good home theater, you become part of the experience. A football player running out of the screen to catch a pass demonstrates this point very effectively.

Explaining why Pioneer chose to use this medium, Michael Fidler, senior vice president, Pioneer Electronics (USA), Inc. says, "As the leaders in the Home Theater marketplace, we wanted to use leading-edge technology in extending the impact of our overall marketing campaign. An interactive demo disk fulfilled that requirement and provided added value by allowing us to convey so much information to a large base of viewers. Since the demo has the ability to print information out on a printer, when the user is done watching the demo, he can leave with a reminder of what he has seen."

CONCLUSION

Hopefully, you've enjoyed this journey through the virtual worlds of the PC-based artist. Regardless of the category presented, we hope you have been left with an appreciation of each artist's individual style. It is the artist's work that humanizes and cushions the too often harsh march of technology forward.

Traditional art forms, such as painting and sculpture, are taught and passed down from mentor to understudy without too great a shift in the general technique. The masters come and go and their work endures safe in a well-established and recognized art form. These PC-based artists, whether they be hobbyists, students, or professionals, are all pioneering new uses of computers and software. Through the beauty of their work, it is our hope that more people will be inspired to produce their own computer graphics.

If hundreds of years from now when somebody digs up an old PC and finds our *Walkthroughs & Flybys CD,* we hope that when they play it their first words are, "Way cool!"

CONTRIBUTOR LISTINGS

This is a list of all the artists who contributed animations, demos, or programs to *Walkthroughs & Flybys CD*. The list is in alphabetical order by last name (many of these artists are hobbyists who don't work for any particular companies). Fax numbers have been excluded in order to conserve space. No international dialing prefixes have been provided, so hopefully all of the phone numbers listed are in the form one would dial from within that country. The name of each artist's best piece is included as the last line in the listing.

Anders Aldengård
Rigstavägen 1039
860 35 Söråker
Sweden
Tel.: 060-41582
Crystal Dream

Jeff Alu
2535 Chestnut Ave.
Orange, CA 92667
USA
Tel.: 714-633-8051
CompuServe: 70733,1445
CCDOBJCT.FLI

Bob Bennett
Autodesk Corporation
2320 Marinship Way
Sausalito, CA 94965
USA
KRAMER.FLI

Niko Boese
Troubadix Studio
Rotdornallee 16
2000 Hamburg 71
Germany
Tel.: 04065-69980
BIGDEMO Music

Michele Bousquet
Many Worlds Productions
CompuServe: 100032,1622
DUDE.FLI

Stephen Brabbins
Digital Image
8 Park Drive
Bingley, W. Yorkshire
BD16 3DF
UK
Tel.: 0274-551007
CompuServe: 100015,411
KIDZ640.EXE

Simon Browne
Parallel Universe
63 Mount Road
Bexleyheath, Kent
DA6 8JS
UK
Tel.: 081-304-0350
DOLPHIN.FLC

Rae Callender
Animated Systems & Design
1900 Embarcadero Rd. #111
Palo Alto, CA 94303
USA
Tel.: 415-424-8586
Pioneer Demo

Charles Carr
30497 Lilac Road
Valley Center, CA 92082
USA
Tel.: 619-749-8229
3D House

Jamie Clay
Autodesk Corporation
2320 Marinship Way
Sausalito, CA 94965
USA
KRAMER.FLI

Andy Dean
Quad Production Company
Cherry Hinton Road
Cambridge, CB1 4DH
UK
Tel.: 0223-413711
Toshiba T2000 Demo

Graeme Devine
Trilobyte
P.O. Box 1412
Jacksonville, OR 97530
USA
Tel.: 503-899-1113
CompuServe: 72330,3276
PLAY80 SVGA FLC Player

Jason Gibbs
Interactive Media Solutions
4 High Street
Twyford, Berks RG10 9AE
UK
Tel.: 0734-344666
CompuServe:100030,53
Xerox Demo

Steve Glauberman
Enlighten
205 North Main Street
Ann Arbor, MI 48104
USA
Tel.: 313-668-6678
CompuServe: 71026,1347
SPCEVENT.EXE

Thomas Guthery IV
Flix Productions
Rt. 1 Box 601
DelValle, TX 78617
USA
Tel.: 512-247-3974
CompuServe: 72740,1326
GUMBY.FLI

Mike Harrison
ORIGIN Systems, Inc.
12940 Research Blvd.
Austin, TX 78750
USA
Tel.: 512-335-5200
Wing Commander II Demo

Magnus Hogdahl
Skarvvagen 7
86100 Timra
Sweden
(46) 013121900

Duke Houston
Houston Graphics
707 Pelton Ave.
Santa Cruz, CA 95060
USA
Tel.: 408-423-6755
MCI-Mail: 501-6754
SK2DEMO.EXE

Tom Hudock
Systemax Computer Graphics
201 E. 87th Street 24E
New York, NY 10128
USA
Tel.: 212-348-8756
CompuServe: 71511,1375
DNEWS002.EXE

Charles Jameson
Silver Tongue Software
343 Central Ave.
Wilmette, IL 60091-1941
USA
Tel.: 708-256-3122
CompuServe: 71350,1014
PEAPOD.EXE

Kenn Jordan
Screen Artists Ltd.
123 Westmead Road
Sutton Surrey
SM1 4JH
UK
Tel.: 081-642-1370

Adam Maitland
Virtual Image Ltd.
Shepperton Studios #57
MIDDX TW17 0QD
UK
Tel.: 0293-862832
Email 100020,255
PERPETUA.FLI

Christian Menard
Starcom
Limburggasse 45
A-9073 Klagenfurt
Austria
Tel.: 0463-296722
Fractal Zoom

Karl Miller
Marketing Systems
P.O. Box 9151
Saskatoon, SK S7K 7E8
Canada
Tel.: 306-975-1030
CompuServe: 73720,2100
MKTSYS2.EXE

Mike Morrison
Software Sorcery
7120 Shoreline Drive #2105
San Diego, CA 92122
USA
Tel.: 619-458-9377
CompuServe: 70413,3450
SUN_EXP.FLI

Michael Mulholland
97 Devonshire Road
Birmingham B20 2PG
UK
Tel.: 021-523-4446
CHESS.FLI

Pat Nessling
The Artwork Exchange
45 The Hyde
Eastbourne, BN21 9BY
UK
Tel.: 0323-507975
"Watch This Space"

Ingo Neumann
Animation & Grafik
Karl-Glaessing-Strasse 5
6200 Wiesbaden
Germany
Tel.: 0611-308-1854
CompuServe:100136,155
SPEAFIRE.FLC

David Nielsen
Ketiv Technology
6601 NE 78th Court #A8
Portland, OR 97218
Tel.: 503-252-3230
ROBOTRK.FLI

Eric Oostendorp
Ultraforce
P.O. Box 63048
3002 JA Rotterdam
The Netherlands
Internet vg12521@si.hhs.nl
VECTDEMO.EXE

Kirt Prchlik
Trik Graphcs Corp.
4612 S. Main Street
South Bend, IN 46614
USA
Tel.: 219-291-7240
LOWLOGO.FLI

Bill Pulver
2916 Barrister Lane
Bowie, MD 20715
USA
Tel.: 301-464-3648
CompuServe: 70405,1152
WINE.EXE

Tom Pytel
Renaissance
1947 65th Street
Brooklyn, NY 11204
USA
Tel.: 718-837-4143
AMNESIA.EXE

Ed Rochelle
Vivid Images
629 Dutch Neck Road
E. Windsor, NJ 08520
USA
Tel.: 609-443-1845
CompuServe: 72007,1603
VIVIDSHP.FLI

Greg St. George
4220 Glengary Ct.
Hanover Park, IL 60103
USA
CompuServe:76067,2532
KICKME.FLI

Bryan St. Germain
Griffin Studios
4622 Dark Hollow Road
Medford, OR 97501
USA
Tel.: 503-772-6833
CompuServe: 76216,2675
PUZZLE.EXE

Randale Sechrest, M.D.
Medical Multimedia Group
308 Lousiana Avenue
Libby, MT 59923
USA
Tel.: 406-293-6262
CompuServe: 71131,602
BACK.EXE

Philip Shaddock
2715 W. 2nd Ave
Vancouver, BC V6K 1K2
Canada
Tel.: 604-732-9917
CompuServe: 70274,2146
DEMOFLUK.EXE

Phil Shatz
Screen Artists Ltd.
123 Westmead Road
Sutton Surrey SM1 4JH
UK
Tel.: 081-642-1370
CompuServe:76470,233
ICL 92 Collection

Paul Smith
201 West Stassney #232
Austin, TX 78745
USA
Gumby's Sculptor

Robert Stein III
Anigraf/x
P.O. Box 1715
Jacksonville, OR 97530
USA
Tel.: 503-772-6525
CYBERNET.FLI

Erik Stridell
Cascada
Rotevagen
S-735 33 Surahammar
Sweden
Tel.: (0220) 33489
CRONOLOG.EXE

Adrian Sutton
Multimedia Music Company
7 Woodlands
London SE13 6TZ
UK
Tel.: 081-698-0534
ICL 92 Collection Soundtrack

Samuli Syvahuoko
Future Crew
Hiiralantie 27a
02160 Espoo
Finland
Tel.: 90-427-477
Internet:
jtheinon@cc.helsinki.fi
UNREAL.EXE

Micha Van Der Meer
Witan
P.O. Box 113
2100 AC Heemstede
Holland
Tel.: 23289684
Internet:
witan@utopia.hacktic.nl

Frank Vivirito
Technical Designs
8231 No Boundary Rd.
Baltimore, MD 21222
USA
Tel.: 301-282-5286
CompuServe:72570,2754
FLIGHT.EXE

Peter White
Troubadix Studio
Rotdornallee 16
2000 Hamburg 71
Germany
Tel.: 04065-69980
BIGDEMO Music

Gary Yost
c/o Autodesk Corporation
2320 Marinship Way
Sausalito, CA 94965
USA
CompuServe:76702,413

APPENDIX B

TROUBLESHOOTING

This section of *Walkthroughs & Flybys CD* is designed to help you solve the most common problems that will probably arise. Because these programs require such relatively vast system resources, certain anomalies are bound to occur. If a particular demo does hang your system, generally you should try to run it again immediately after restarting your computer. On occasion, certain demos may fail to release all the memory areas they occupied upon terminating, and a fresh boot will clear up the situation. In the event your circumstances are more dire, please scan the headings below to see if they shed any light on your problem.

The most common problem we expect people to have will be because their systems have insufficient DOS memory to run certain demos. A very important piece of information that very few people seem to know is that the Microsoft CDROM extension program, MSCDEX.EXE, will load a large part of itself into EMS memory if you add a /E to the end of the line in your AUTOEXEC.BAT file. If you still don't have enough memory after trying this, consider purchasing QEMM from Quarterdeck.

PROBLEMS LOADING THE MENU SYSTEM

Executing WF.BAT after installation gives the following error message:

```
Out of environment space
This computer does not have sufficient DOS environment space free for
the Walkthroughs & Flybys CD menu system to operate. Please allocate
at least 25 additional bytes of environment space. The easiest way to do
this is by adding the following line to your CONFIG.SYS file and then
rebooting.

  SHELL = C:\COMMAND.COM /E:### /p

For DOS 3.1 replace ### with the number of 16-byte blocks you require.
For 3.2 and up, replace ### with the actual number of bytes.
```

As the error message states, the *Walkthroughs & Flybys CD* menu system uses DOS environment variables to store data. On many computers, the environment already may be completely in use. Rather than have the menu system fail, WF.BAT first checks to be sure that sufficient environment space exists before the menu system is loaded.

Increasing the size of your DOS environment requires editing your CONFIG.SYS file. If your system already has a line that sets the size of the environment using the SHELL command, just increase the amount of memory specified by the /E: parameter. If your system doesn't have a line starting with SHELL in your CONFIG.SYS file, then just add the following to it:

```
SHELL=C:\COMMAND.COM /e:300
```

This will increase the size of your DOS environment from the default of 256 characters to 300.

Not enough environment from within Windows.

If you try to execute WF.BAT from inside of Microsoft Windows, you are very likely to get the "out of environment space" error message. When Windows creates a DOS session, it generally leaves no free characters for the DOS environment. Installing the *Walkthroughs & Flybys CD* or running the menu system from inside of Windows is not recommended.

PROBLEMS WITH THE BIGDEMO

The BIGDEMO uses the MMPLAY.EXE program from Creative Labs to play Autodesk Animator format FLI files concurrently with digitized and sequenced music. After extensive testing with several versions of MMPLAY and the associated driver files, we are confident that the BIGDEMO will run on your system without error. The BIGDEMO has been tested on the following audio cards:

Creative Labs Inc.	Sound Blaster
	Sound Blaster Pro
	Sound Blaster 16 ASP
Media Vision	Pro Audio Spectrum
ATI Technologies	Stereo F/X

Some common problems that we encountered are listed in the following text, along with our recommended path to their resolution.

When running on a Sound Blaster Pro Multimedia Upgrade Kit (MMUK), the music often terminates while the graphics continue to play. Occasionally, the graphics play for a few seconds with no music at all.

Different versions of MMPLAY run scripts at different speeds. The BIGDEMO is timed for the VideoBlaster version of MMPLAY that is included on the CD. After thorough testing, it has proved to be the most reliable. If you always choose Option 2 to install the drivers from the CD, the BIGDEMO will run perfectly in sync.

The graphics run but you can't hear any sound.

As with any PC-related problem, check the cables first. Be sure your speaker cables are plugged into the correct jack by running the Sound Blaster diagnostic software. If you hear music when you run the diagnostics, you know your Sound Blaster is installed correctly.

Some Sound Blaster cards have on-board mixers, so be sure your volume levels are set high enough to hear the music. Sound Blaster Pro users should refer to their manuals for instructions on using SBP-MIX.EXE or SBP-SET.EXE to adjust these levels.

The music and graphics play for a time before garbage appears on the screen. Even though the image is corrupted, the graphics and music continue to play.

Your system doesn't have enough free DOS memory to run the BIGDEMO. After you chose to run the BIGDEMO, the first screen advised you that you needed 520K of free memory. The amount of available memory was then displayed. To get this error, you must have ignored the warning and decided to proceed anyway.

To resolve this problem you must either load fewer device drivers and resident utilities or load them into high memory. To facilitate this, we strongly recommend that you purchase QEMM from Quarterdeck to serve as your memory manager. The OPTIMIZE program will analyze your system and correctly configure it for you with a minimum of effort. Trying to make the most of your DOS memory can be a real nightmare without this product.

BIGDEMO fails to run, displaying one of the following (or a similar) error message:

```
SBFMDRV: Error 0001: Sound Blaster Pro does not exist at the I/O address
specified.
MMPLAY: Interrupt error, Sound Blaster or Video Blaster not found or
turned off
```

The value of either the I/O address or the interrupt setting (IRQ) specified in the BLASTER environment string does not match the configuration of your card. You will get this message when your Sound Blaster is either incorrectly installed or you chose the wrong values when you tried to install the drivers for the BIGDEMO. MMPLAY.EXE looks at the contents of BLASTER to see how the card is configured. If it can't initialize the sound card based on the settings it finds in BLASTER, this error message is displayed. If you have a standard Sound Blaster or compatible card, don't worry that this error message refers to a Sound Blaster Pro or Video Blaster. The MMPLAY program and drivers will work just fine on these lower spec cards.

To resolve this problem, you should install the Sound Blaster driver files from the CD when you start the BIGDEMO. This installation procedure will overwrite the values of your SOUND and BLASTER environment variables. This way you can specify the correct I/O address and IRQ setting that matches your card, ensuring that the MMPLAY will run without failure. Note that these new drivers will be copied into the \WF subdirectory and, therefore, will not permanently alter your existing configuration. Once you reboot, your system will be returned to its original settings.

To install the Sound Blaster drivers from the CD, you will need to know the I/O address and the interrupt (IRQ) settings for your audio card. If you don't know this information, you will have to run the diagnostic/setup program provided by your manufacturer to find out what they are. (On the Sound Blaster Pro, run TEST-SBP.EXE to get this information.) The Sound Blaster, Sound Blaster Pro, and the ATI Stereo F/X all default to an I/O address of 220 Hex and IRQ 7. The Media Vision Pro Audio Spectrum and the Sound Blaster 16 ASP default to I/O address 220 Hex and IRQ 5.

Media Vision Pro Audio Spectrum

You must run the Media Vision INSTALL.EXE program to activate the Sound Blaster emulation of the Pro Audio Spectrum card. Even though the INSTALL.EXE program may inform you that Sound Blaster emulation is set for IRQ 7, you might find that it is actually on IRQ 5. In our experience, this has consistently been the case. If you have removed your Pro Audio Spectrum card and have just reinstalled it, you must run the program \SPECTRUM\INSTALL.EXE to reinitialize the Sound Blaster emulation.

ATI Stereo F/X

Users of this card must first install the software in order to initialize Sound Blaster emulation. As mentioned above, the card defaults to I/O address 220 and IRQ 7.

MAKING A BOOT DISK

Six of the most amazing demos for the Sound Blaster (Facts of Life, FISHTRO, UNREAL, PANIC, Wing Commander II, and CRONOLOG) require more than 580K of free DOS memory to run. Because most PCs with CD-ROM drives installed have less than this amount free, we devised the following procedure to let you run these amazing demos from your hard disk without any modifications to the CONFIG.SYS or AUTOEXEC.BAT files. The **Make a Boot Disk** procedure will give PCs running DOS 5.0 around 617K of free DOS memory. If you are running an earlier version of DOS, we recommend that you purchase either QEMM from Quarterdeck or 386-to-the-Max from Qualitas in order to get enough free memory to see these demos on your system. Here is a description of what this procedure does:

1. Formats a floppy in the A drive with FORMAT /S to create a bootable system disk.

2. Copies the HIMEM.SYS and EMM386.EXE files to the floppy so they can be accessed as the PC boots.

3. Creates the following CONFIG.SYS file on the floppy to load DOS into high memory. A listing of this file and a description of each line follows.

CONFIG.SYS
```
device=himem.sys
dos=high,umb
device=emm386.exe 1024 ram frame=e000
```

The first line loads HIMEM.SYS, the Microsoft device driver that allows you to load drivers above 640K. The DOS=HIGH,UMB tells DOS to use this high memory area. It also tells DOS to use EMM386.EXE to load itself into the UMB (Upper Memory Block). The DEVICE=EMM386.EXE statement loads the Microsoft extended memory manager. It converts 1,024,000 bytes of extended memory in your computer into 1,024,000 bytes of expanded memory that can be used for storing various programs and device drivers, so they don't end up in the 640K address space.

4. Creates the following AUTOEXEC.BAT file on the floppy:

AUTOEXEC.BAT
```
pause
prompt $p$g
path=c:\dos
mem
pause
set t=C:
call auto floppy.mdf
@echo off
echo You can reload the menu system from this floppy by entering WF
```

The path statement defines the directory names for important locations on your hard disk. The DOS directory is needed so the program MEM will work. The line MEM will display on the screen how much memory is actually free after your PC has booted. The line SET T=C: is required so the menu system on the floppy knows which hard disk drive has the demos. CALL AUTO FLOPPY.MDF loads the Automenu application that actually plays the demos from your hard disk. The final line prints a reminder to the screen of how to restart the floppy menu system when you quit.

5. After the boot floppy is created, the six memory-hungry demos are copied to a \WFTEMP subdirectory on your hard disk.

6. The final step in the procedure creates the menu system on the floppy for playing these demos from the hard disk.

If you want to start this procedure, please choose **Make a boot disk with this menu system installed** option from the *Walkthroughs & Flybys CD* main menu.

PROBLEMS WITH OTHER DEMOS

PANIC fails to load.
Wing Commander II crashes after the orchestra.

These demos require expanded memory or EMS. If you are using DOS 5.0 with HIMEM.SYS, be sure to add the EMM386.EXE device driver to your CONFIG.SYS file. If you don't want to change your CONFIG.SYS file, choose the **Make a Boot Disk** option to play these demos.

FISHTRO music dies after 5 seconds.

You've chosen the wrong IRQ setting or I/O address for your Sound Blaster.

Crystal Dream

The music dies after 2 seconds on **Crystal Dream** when run on a Sound Blaster 16 card. We have been unable to find a fix for this problem. Crystal runs fine on all of the other Sound Blaster and compatible cards.

AMNESIA

This is the only executable demonstration on *Walkthroughs & Flybys CD* that is not accessible through the menu system. Because this program runs in protected mode it requires a clean boot of your machine with no memory management software installed. If you want to run Amnesia follow these steps:

1. Copy the file \SBDEMOS\RENAISSA\AMNESIA.EXE to your hard disk.
2. Create a boot disk by choosing the **Make Boot Disk** option from the main menu. Choose N when asked whether you want to copy files to your hard disk. This way the process will be aborted once the boot floppy has been created.
3. Quit the *Walkthroughs & Flybys CD* menu system and load the CONFIG.SYS file into an editor such as EDIT.EXE that comes with DOS 5.0.
4. Put the letters REM in front of the first line so that it reads as such:
   REM DEVICE=HIMEM.SYS
5. Save the file and reboot your PC from the boot floppy. You should be able to run Amnesia with no problems.

Tip: If you have trouble running a sequence of demos, quit the program and turn off your computer for 10–15 seconds. Then run the problem demo again. Turning off the computer will clear its memory.

APPENDIX C

SOURCES

The following products are mentioned in the text of this book. For the most part, they played an important role in the development of one or many of the pieces of art in the collection. Unless otherwise noted, all of these addresses are in the United States.

3D Studio, Animator Pro

Autodesk Corporation
2320 Marinship Way
Sausalito, CA 94965
Tel.: 415-332-2344
Fax: 415-331-8093
CompuServe: GO ASOFT

The vast majority of the 3-D animations included on the accompanying CD-ROM were created with Autodesk 3D Studio. Animator Pro is a companion program for editing flic files.

Domark Virtual Reality Toolkit

Domark, Inc.
1900 South Norfolk St. #202
San Mateo, CA 94403
USA
Tel.: 415-513-8929
Fax: 415-571-0437

Domark Software Ltd.
51-57 Lacy Road
Putney, London SW15 1PR
UK
Tel.: 081-780-2222

This inexpensive package creates 3-D worlds the user can move through interactively with a mouse. In the United Kingdom, it is sold under the name of the Domark 3D Construction Kit.

GRASP

Paul Mace Software
400 Williamson Way
Ashland, OR 97520
Tel.: 503-488-0224
Fax: 503-488-1549
BBS: 503-482-7435
CompuServe: GO GRASP

Most of the demos on the *Walkthroughs & Flybys CD* were produced with GRASP. The acronym GRaphic Animation System for Professionals says it all. Get *Multimedia Creations* by Phil Shaddock from Waite Group Press for more information on this fantastic program.

Mannequin

HUMANCAD
1800 Walt Whitman Road
Melville, NY 11747
Tel.: 516-752-3568
Fax: 516-752-3507

Mannequin is the first ergonomic design program to accurately model the human figure. It creates anatomically correct 3-D models of people for use with popular CAD software.

Deluxe Paint II Enhanced, Deluxe Paint Animation

Electronic Arts
1450 Fashion Island Blvd.
San Mateo, CA 94404
Tel.: 415-571-7171
Fax: 415-570-5137

Leaders in the production of home entertainment software for the PC, this company also publishes these two popular drawing programs.

The Sound Blaster

Creative Labs Inc.
1901 McCarthy Blvd.
Milpitas, CA 95035
Tel.: 408-428-6600
Fax: 408-428-6611

The Sound Blaster is the leading add-in audio card for the PC.

Video Electronics Standards Association (VESA)

1330 South Bascom Avenue, Suite D
San Jose, CA 95128-4502

VESA publishes standards governing various aspects of PC graphics compatibility.

Automenu

Magee Enterprises, Inc.
Post Office Box 1587
Norcross, GA 30091
Tel.: 404-446-6611
Fax: 404-368-0719
BBS: 404-446-6650
CompuServe: 76004,1541 or 70167,2200

Automenu is the development system that was used to create the interface for the vast range of programs on the *Walkthroughs & Flybys* CD-ROM.

BATCOM

Wenham Software Co.
5 Burley Street
Wenham, MA 01984
Tel.: 508-774-7036

This batch file compiler proved to be indispensable in the course of this project. It was used to create the installation program for *Walkthroughs & Flybys CD*.

Fractint, Fractint for Windows

Stone Soup Group
CompuServe: GO COMART

Fractint is the leading shareware fractal generation program. Get The Waite Group's *Fractal Creations* for more!

IPAS Boutique

The Yost Group Inc. &
Schrieber Instruments
Tel.: 800-368-4727
Tel.: 303-757-3052
Fax: 303-759-0928
CompuServe: GO ASOFT

The IPAS Boutique is a collection of external processes for extending the capabilities of Autodesk 3D Studio.

VISTAPRO

Virtual Reality Labs Inc.
2341 Ganador Court
San Luis Obispo, CA 93401
BBS: 805-781-2256
Tel.: 805-545-8515
CompuServe: GO VRLI

VISTAPRO is a computer-aided art program that allows PC users to quickly produce electronic landscapes of stunning realism. When used with the Make Path Flight Director, creating animated fly-throughs is a snap.

The Human Figure in Motion

Eadweard Muybridge
New York: Dover Publications Inc., 1955
ISBN 0-486-20204-6

This book contains over 4,700 photographs from the Muybridge Collection chosen for their value to artists, doctors, and researchers.

DISC MAP AND
DIRECTORY CONTENTS

In order to help you find particular files, the entire contents of the disc are listed below. The directory tree shown in Table D-1 contains information only down to the third directory level where demos are organized by artist. For more information on the contents of any given directory, refer to that heading in the pages that follow.

Table D-1 Directory map of *Walkthroughs & Flybys CD*

Directory	Description
\	**1** Root Directory
+ - - -DEMOS	**2** Demos for the PC created almost entirely with GRASP
+ - - -ASDI	**3** Animated Systems & Design Inc., Palo Alto, CA, USA
+ - - -CARR	**4** Charles Carr, Valley Center, CA, USA
+ - - -DIGIT_I	**5** Digital Image Ltd., Bingley, West Yorkshire, UK
+ - - -ENLIGHTE	**6** Enlighten, Ann Arbor, MI, USA
+ - - -FLIX	**7** FLIX Productions, DelValle, TX, USA
+ - - -GRIFFIN	**8** Griffin Studios, Medford, OR, USA
+ - - -HOUSTON	**9** Houston Graphics, Santa Cruz, CA, USA
+ - - -IMS	**10** Interactive Media Solutions, Twyford, Berkshire, UK
+ - - -MARKETSY	**11** Marketing Systems, Saskatoon, SK, Canada
+ - - -MEDICALM	**12** Medical Multimedia Group, Libby, MT USA

| +---NESSLING	**13** Pat Nessling, Eastbourne, Sussex, UK
| +---PULVER	**14** Bill Pulver, Bowie, MD, USA
| +---SARTISTS	**15** Screen Artists Ltd., Sutton, Surrey, UK
| +---SHADDOCK	**16** Philip Shaddock, Vancouver, BC, Canada
| +---SILVER_T	**17** Silver Tongue Software, Wilmette, IL, USA
| \---SYSTEMAX	**18** Systemax Computer Graphics, New York, NY, USA
+---FLIC	**19** Autodesk flic animations not categorized by artist
| +---FLC	**20** SuperVGA animations in the FLC format
| +---FLI	**21** Standard VGA animations in the FLI format
| \---IPAS	**22** FLI files and GIF pictures regarding 3D Studio IPAS
+---PROGRAMS	**23** The menu system and all the supporting utilities
\---SBDEMOS	**24** Demos for the Sound Blaster
+---BIGDEMO	**25** Peter White, Niko Boese, and Phil Shatz
+---CASCADA	**26** Cascada, Surahammer, Sweden
+---FUTURE_C	**27** The Future Crew, Espoo, Finland
+---ORIGIN	**28** ORIGIN Systems, Austin, TX, USA
+---RENAISSA	**29** Renaissance, Brooklyn, NY, USA
+---STARCOM	**30** Starcom CDROM, Klangenfurt, Austria
+---TRITON	**31** Triton, Söråker, Sweden
+---ULTRA_FO	**32** Ultraforce Software Dev., Rotterdam, Holland
\---WITAN	**33** Witan, Heemstede, Holland

1 Root Directory

```
\
INSTALL.EXE      Installs the menu system on your hard disk.
TREEINFO.NCD     A directory tree listing for users of Norton Change
                 Directory.
```

2 Demos for the PC created almost entirely with GRASP

\DEMOS
There are no files in this subdirectory. Demos by particular groups are located in the subdirectories off this branch.

3 Animated Systems & Design Inc., Palo Alto, CA, USA

\DEMOS\ASDI

PIONEER.EXE	Demo for Pioneer Home Theater products.
ASDI.EXE	A VGA sampler of various demos created by this team.

4 Charles Carr, Valley Center, CA, USA

\DEMOS\CARR

3DHOUSE2.BAT	Interactive walkthrough of a house and grounds created with Domark Virtual Reality Studio.

5 Digital Image Ltd., Bingley, West Yorkshire, UK

\DEMOS\DIGIT_I

The demos from Digital Image were created using Topaz from GSL Software Labs to generate true-color Targa files, which were then assembled into animations using GRASP.

HSEGOLD.EXE	Logo for the Health and Safety Executive.
KIDZ640.EXE	Moving video is mapped to the sides of rotating block.
POUND640.EXE	A rotating UK pound sign.
TAP.EXE	A Digital Image logo of a water faucet.

6 Enlighten, Ann Arbor, MI, USA

\DEMOS\ENLIGHTE

ENLCARD.EXE	Excellent demo that shows a number of innovative ways to get rid of leftover fruitcake.
SPCEVENT.EXE	Software Publishing Corporation's Event on a Disk.
SCDEMO.EXE	Computer Associates SuperCalc 5 Demo.
DBFDEMO.EXE	Computer Associates dbFast Ver 2.0.
CLIPDEMO.EXE	Computer Associates Clipper.
READEMO.EXE	Computer Associates Realizer.
TXTDEMO.EXE	Computer Associates Textor.
ACPDEMO.EXE	Computer Associates ACCPAC Plus.
CBVDEMO.EXE	Computer Associates CobolVision.

7 FLIX Productions, DelValle, TX, USA

\DEMOS\FLIX

AWORDS.EXE   Animated Words teaches young children to read.

8 Griffin Studios, Medford, OR, USA

\DEMOS\GRIFFIN

PUZZLE.EXE   Shows a number of excellent uses for PC demos. Includes a game.

9 Houston Graphics, Santa Cruz, CA, USA

\DEMOS\HOUSTON

SK2DEMO.EXE   Borland's Sidekick II demo.
SL25DEMO.EXE   Everex SL25 Monochromatic demo.
XMASCARD.EXE   Christmas card created for Paul Mace Software.

10 Interactive Media Solutions, Twyford, Berkshire, UK

There are eight excellent demos by this group which are located in subdirectories off \DEMOS\IMS.

CU.EXE   Commercial Union demonstration.
IIT.EXE   Integrated Information Technology Europe's Math Coprocessor demo.
XD.EXE   Integrated Information Technology Europe's Xtra Drive demo.
OAG.EXE   Official Airlines Guide "To Bahrain and Back or Bust" demo.
QUANTUM.EXE   Thomas Cook "Making the Most of Travel Information" demo.
VICTOR1.EXE   Victor Technologies "A Company with a History" demo.
VLSAMPLE.EXE   Videologic Product Sampler demo.
START.EXE   Xerox Engineering Systems 8810 Laser Plotter demo.

11 Marketing Systems, Saskatoon, SK, Canada

\DEMOS\MARKETSY

MARKETSY.EXE   Samples from various projects that feature some clever illustrations.

MKTSY2.EXE   Chromagraphics and Marketing Systems offer various services.

12 Medical Multimedia Group, Libby, MT USA

\DEMOS\MEDICALM

ROUNDS.EXE   Montana Grand Rounds \ Healthcon's Thumb Deformity demo.

BACK.EXE   Patient's Guide to Lower Back Pain.

13 Pat Nessling, Eastbourne, Sussex, UK

\DEMOS\NESSLING

DEMO1\DEMO.BAT "Wormville" demo in DeluxePaint Animation.

DEMO2\DEMO.BAT "Watch This Space" demo.

14 Bill Pulver, Bowie, MD, USA

\DEMOS\PULVER

WINE.EXE   The modeling for this flyby was created with AutoCAD. Big-D was used for the rendering.

15 Screen Artists Ltd., Sutton, Surrey, UK

\DEMOS\SARTISTS

92COL.BAT   The ICL 92 Collection demo is 27MB of graphics and 5:22 of audio.

ICLPS.EXE   ICL "People Working Together" demo.

T2000.EXE   Toshiba T2000 demo done with The Quad Production Company.

16 Philip Shaddock, Vancouver, BC, Canada

DEMOFLUK.EXE   John Fluke 9110FT demo.

17 Silver Tongue Software, Wilmette, IL, USA

VGA\START.BAT   Standard VGA kiosk application for floppy disk distribution.

SVGA\START.BAT   SuperVGA Peapod kiosk application.

18 Systemax Computer Graphics, New York, NY, USA

\DEMOS\SYSTEMAX

DNEWS002.EXE   DiscNews Volume 2 — A company newsletter on floppy disk.

GREET91.EXE   A Christmas greeting card.

19 Autodesk flic animations not categorized by artist

\FLIC

There are no files in this subdirectory. Animations in the Autodesk flic format are located in the three subdirectories off this branch.

20 SuperVGA animations in the FLC format

\FLIC\FLC

You will find the following files in the \FLIC\FLC directory. All of these animations are in 640x480 screen resolution. The Trilobyte Flick and Groovie Player used to display these animations can be found in the file \PROGRAMS\PLAY.EXE.

File Name	Creator	Size (K)
ATI_JET.FLC	Screen Artists	8,911
BLOB.FLC	Bill Pulver	2,900
DISINT.FLC	Yost Group	7,776
DOLPHIN.FLC	Simon Browne	8,784
EXPLCYL.FLC	Yost Group	5,493
FISH.FLC	Simon Browne	1,995
FWORKS1.FLC	Yost Group	6,574
HEAD1.FLC	Simon Browne	5,582
MANTA.FLC	Yost Group	1,580
RELFECTS.FLC	Ingo Neumann	4,210

ROOM.FLC	Simon Browne	4,054
SCALE01.FLC	AniGrafx	1,298
SKULL.FLC	AniGrafx	538
SPEAFIRE.FLC	Ingo Neumann	13,930
SWIM.FLC	AniGrafx	2,067
WALK.FLC	Screen Artists	3,722
WARP_ICE.FLC	Yost Group	4,655

21 Standard VGA animations in the FLI format

\FLIC\FLI

File Name	Creator	Size (K)
1988EG4.FLI	Jeff Alu	335
3DEYE.FLI	Jeff Alu	335
3DSLOGO.FLI	Autodesk	526
A3DSDEMO.FLI	Autodesk	720
AAAUTO.FLI	Autodesk	776
AAWORLD.FLI	Autodesk	315
ADMOD.FLI	Autodesk	788
AMBSUPRI.FLI	Autodesk	1,679
ASLAMP.FLI	Autodesk	1,852
ATI_COL.FLI	Screen Artists	1,370
ATI_JET.FLI	Screen Artists	2,962
BALL2.FLI	Autodesk	200
BARBER.FLI	Screen Artists	1,009
BIRD5.FLI	Autodesk	1,175
BLIND.FLI	Autodesk	1,049
BOOKSPIN.FLI	Autodesk	1,497
BOUNCE.FLI	Autodesk	47
BRIDGFLY.FLI	Autodesk	5,023
BRROTOR.FLI	Autodesk	80
BZOOM320.FLI	Tom Guthery	1,045
CANADA2.FLI	Autodesk	1,129
CARBOARD.FLI	Autodesk	1,563
CARS.FLI	Autodesk	9,823
CCDOBJC2.FLI	Jeff Alu	4,944
CCDOBJCT.FLI	Jeff Alu	272

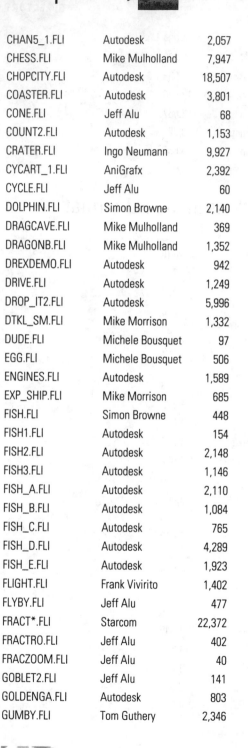

CHAN5_1.FLI	Autodesk	2,057
CHESS.FLI	Mike Mulholland	7,947
CHOPCITY.FLI	Autodesk	18,507
COASTER.FLI	Autodesk	3,801
CONE.FLI	Jeff Alu	68
COUNT2.FLI	Autodesk	1,153
CRATER.FLI	Ingo Neumann	9,927
CYCART_1.FLI	AniGrafx	2,392
CYCLE.FLI	Jeff Alu	60
DOLPHIN.FLI	Simon Browne	2,140
DRAGCAVE.FLI	Mike Mulholland	369
DRAGONB.FLI	Mike Mulholland	1,352
DREXDEMO.FLI	Autodesk	942
DRIVE.FLI	Autodesk	1,249
DROP_IT2.FLI	Autodesk	5,996
DTKL_SM.FLI	Mike Morrison	1,332
DUDE.FLI	Michele Bousquet	97
EGG.FLI	Michele Bousquet	506
ENGINES.FLI	Autodesk	1,589
EXP_SHIP.FLI	Mike Morrison	685
FISH.FLI	Simon Browne	448
FISH1.FLI	Autodesk	154
FISH2.FLI	Autodesk	2,148
FISH3.FLI	Autodesk	1,146
FISH_A.FLI	Autodesk	2,110
FISH_B.FLI	Autodesk	1,084
FISH_C.FLI	Autodesk	765
FISH_D.FLI	Autodesk	4,289
FISH_E.FLI	Autodesk	1,923
FLIGHT.FLI	Frank Vivirito	1,402
FLYBY.FLI	Jeff Alu	477
FRACT*.FLI	Starcom	22,372
FRACTRO.FLI	Jeff Alu	402
FRACZOOM.FLI	Jeff Alu	40
GOBLET2.FLI	Jeff Alu	141
GOLDENGA.FLI	Autodesk	803
GUMBY.FLI	Tom Guthery	2,346

HEAD1.FLI	Simon Browne	1,387
ICL.FLI	Screen Artists	7,519
ICL_16.FLI	Screen Artists	880
KICKME.FLI	Greg St. George	2,221
KRAMER.FLI	Autodesk	29,008
KRAMER2.FLI	Autodesk	6,204
LOGO.FLI	Autodesk	1,118
LOWLOGO.FLI	Low Associates	308
MALLFLY.FLI	Autodesk	1,446
MANRUN.FLI	Autodesk	2,363
MIS_STRK.FLI	Mike Morrison	1,213
MMPROP.FLI	Autodesk	1,511
MOLECULE.FLI	Autodesk	1,157
MONFLI.FLI	Jeff Alu	634
MSH.FLI	Jeff Alu	662
MWP.FLI	Michele Bousquet	428
NEWTONLO.FLI	Autodesk	1,294
NIMBUS.FLI	Screen Artists	11,333
PERPETUA.FLI	Virtual Image	14,794
PIPE.FLI	Autodesk	3,337
PLANET.FLI	Autodesk	212
PLANT.FLI	Autodesk	5,067
PLASMA.FLI	Autodesk	104
PLAYROOM.FLI	AniGrafx	960
PROBE.FLI	Mike Morrison	725
PROP.FLI	Autodesk	4,412
ROBOTRK.FLI	David Nielsen	2,362
ROOM.FLI	Simon Browne	1,041
SAILB2.FLI	Paul Unterweiser	1,676
SARTISTS.FLI	Screen Artists	210
SIGNSPIN.FLI	Autodesk	1,910
SPEAFIRE.FLI	Ingo Neumann	3,988
SPROCKET.FLI	Autodesk	3,000
STARGLOB.FLI	Mike Mulholland	1,584
STHELENS.FLI	Autodesk	2,641
STRANGE.FLI	Jeff Alu	327
SUN_EXP.FLI	Mike Morrison	2,145

TWENLOGO.FLI	Autodesk	786
VIVIDSHP.FLI	Vivid Images	1,172
VIV_PRE.FLI	Virtual Image	11,540
WALK.FLI	Screen Artists	836
X29_2A.FLI	Autodesk	397
ZOOM.FLI	Jeff Alu	241

22 FLI files and GIF pictures regarding 3D Studio IPAS

\FLIC\IPAS

All of the following files demonstrate the capabilities to be found in The Yost Group's IPAS boutique.

File Name	Size (K)
BLUR.FLI	114
CLAMP.FLI	271
CRUMPLE.FLI	216
DISINT.FLI	491
EXPLODE.FLI	507
EXPLODE2.FLI	688
EXPLOD_5.FLI	692
FIREWKS.FLI	489
FLARE.FLI	387
GLOW.FLI	271
HILITE.FLI	219
INVOKE.FLI	675
IPASFWRK.FLI	1,154
MELT.FLI	228
MWAVE.FLI	149
MWAVE_1.FLI	151
RAIN.FLI	396
RAIN_2.FLI	243
RESHAPE.FLI	191
SKLINE.FLI	179
SMOKE.FLI	267
SNOW.FLI	391
SPHIFY.FLI	313
SPIRAL01.FLI	300

SPIRAL02.FLI	317
SPURT.FLI	273
STRETCH.FLI	227
TWIST.FLI	227
WATER.FLI	469
XMAS.FLI	10

23 The menu system and all the supporting utilities

\PROGRAMS

File Name	Size (Bytes)	Description
AUTOTEMP.BAT	128	Batch file used by Automenu
AUTOMENU.COM	21,598	Automenu system
AAPLAY.EXE	80,288	Autodesk freely distributable player
FREE.EXE	6,144	Utility to check free disk space
PLAY.EXE	13,755	Trilobyte PLAY80 FLC player
SBDRV.EXE	45,284	Sound Blaster Driver files and MMPLAY in a PKZIP self-extracting archive
WHAT.EXE	3,170	Batch file enhancement program
MEM.COM	347	Utility to display free memory
CREDITS.MDF	1,753	Automenu Menu Definition files
FLC.MDF	434	"
FLCART.MDF	434	"
FLI.MDF	419	"
FLICS.MDF	186	"
FLOPPY.MDF	284	"
FUTURE.MDF	4,048	"
GRASPDE1.MDF	762	"
GRASPDE2.MDF	767	"
GRASPDE3.MDF	783	"
GRASPDE4.MDF	1,833	"
GRASPDEM.MDF	508	"
IPAS.MDF	469	"
MISC.MDF	575	"
MMPLAY.MDF	4,501	"
SBDEMO.MDF	833	"
SETUP.MDF	4,110	"
WF.MDF	385	"

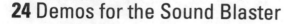

24 Demos for the Sound Blaster

\SBDEMOS

There are no files in this subdirectory. Demos by particular groups are located in the subdirectories off this branch.

25 White, Boese, and Shatz

\SBDEMOS\CPS_COMP

BIGDEMO.SB   The BIGDEMO is an MMPLAY script that accesses over 200MB of graphics and 10MB of VOC and CMF audio.

26 Cascada, Surahammer, Sweden

\SBDEMOS\CASCADA

CRONOLOG.EXE   Cronologia demo features fast graphics and an unconventional style.

27 The Future Crew, Espoo, Finland

\SBDEMOS\FUTURE_C

WFDEMO.EXE   *Walkthroughs & Flybys CD* demo is a marketing demo to promote this product.

FISHTRO.EXE   A digital aquarium demo to promote a party.

PANIC.EXE   The latest large demo by the Future Crew (at the time of this writing).

THEPARTY.EXE   A demo to promote another party.

UNREAL.EXE   The Future Crew's masterpiece.

MENTAL_S.ZIP   Mental Surgery demo includes ASM source code.

SCREAM_T.ZIP   The Scream Tracker music composition program.

28 ORIGIN Systems, Austin, TX, USA

\SBDEMOS\ORIGIN

WING2.EXE   The Wing Commander II demo.

29 Renaissance, Brooklyn, NY, USA

\SBDEMOS\RENAISSA

AMNESIA.EXE   Incredible Sound Blaster demo that runs only if no
memory manager is installed.

30 Starcom CDROM, Klangenfurt, Austria

\SBDEMOS\STARCOM

GO.BAT   This MMPLAY script is a 22MB ride into fractal
worlds.

31 Triton, Söråker, Sweden

\SBDEMOS\TRITON

CRYSTAL.EXE   Crystal Dream demo by Triton.

32 Ultraforce Software Dev., Rotterdam, Holland

\SBDEMOS\ULTRA_FO

VECTDEMO.EXE   High-speed vector animation with real-time shading
of many objects.

33 Witan, Heemstede, Holland

\SBDEMOS\WITAN

FACTS.EXE   The "Facts of Life" demo has fantastic music.

INDEX